DISCOVERING U.S. HISTORY

World War I and the Roaring Twenties

1914–1928

DISCOVERING U.S. HISTORY

DISCOVERING U.S. HISTORY

World War I and the Roaring Twenties 1914–1928

Tim McNeese

Consulting Editor: Richard Jensen, Ph.D.

CHELSEA HOUSE
PUBLISHERS
An imprint of Infobase Publishing

WORLD WAR I AND THE ROARING TWENTIES: 1914–1928

Chelsea House
An imprint of Infobase Publishing
132 West 31st Street
New York NY 10001

Library of Congress Cataloging-in-Publication Data
McNeese, Tim.
 World War I and the Roaring Twenties, 1914–1928 / by Tim McNeese.
   p. cm. — (Discovering U.S. history)
 Includes bibliographical references and index.
 ISBN 978-1-60413-356-1 (hardcover)
 1. World War, 1914–1918—United States—Juvenile literature. 2. United States—History—1913–1921—Juvenile literature. 3. United States—Social life and customs—1918–1945—Juvenile literature. 4. United States—Social conditions—1918–1932—Juvenile literature. 5. Nineteen twenties—Juvenile literature. I. Title. II. Series.

 D619.M3843 2009
 940.3—dc22

                    2009015011

The Discovering U.S. History series was produced for Chelsea House by Bender Richardson White, Uxbridge, UK

Editors: Lionel Bender and Susan Malyan
Designer and Picture Researcher: Ben White
Production: Kim Richardson
Maps and graphics: Stefan Chabluk

Cover printed by Bang Printing, Brainerd, MN
Book printed and bound by Bang Printing, Brainerd, MN
Date printed: April 2010
Printed in the United States of America

10 9 8 7 6 5 4 3 2 1

Contents

Introduction

A New Order

As he prepared to depart New York City on the morning of December 4, 1918, he was showered with a snowy cascade of confetti and support from well-wishers. Riding in an open touring car down the streets of the city, President Woodrow Wilson, tall and slender, top hat firmly in place, then repeatedly tipped to the crowd, was the hero of the American people. The war was over. For more than four years, beginning in June of 1914, the nations of Europe had engaged in a bloody struggle to rearrange the balance of power, both on the continent and around the world. Britain, France, Italy, and a host of lesser allies, including far-away Japan and British colonies such as South Africa, Canada, and Australia, had fought around the globe against those nations known as the Central Powers, led by Germany and the Austro-Hungarian Empire. Almost every nation in Europe had become engulfed in a conflict that quickly became known as the Great War.

Initially the United States had managed to steer clear of the war, with President Wilson declaring that his country and his countrymen would remain neutral. For more than two-and-a-half years, Americans had stayed out of the fight. Yet neutrality had often proved difficult. German submarines engaged in unrestricted warfare, attacking unarmed civilian vessels, including merchant ships and passenger liners. Americans had sometimes been victims of such attacks. With each sinking, the Germans became more sinister to the people of the United States, while the Allies, especially Great Britain, appeared beleaguered. Americans, including Wilson himself, were ultimately drawn from their neutrality, and the United States entered the war in the spring of 1917.

Shifting the Balance of Power

Although late, the entry of the United States into the European theater of war came as a Godsend to the Allies. The previous years of conflict had worn out the fighting forces on both sides. Hundreds of thousands of British, French, Italian, German, Austrian, and Russian soldiers had been shot to ribbons by heavy machine gun fire, poisoned by gas attack, bombed from the air, and cut down by disease. The rural landscapes of Italy, France, and other regions of Europe had been devastated by war. Billions had been spent on the great conflagration, the most destructive conflict in the history of humankind to that time. But during the final 18 months of the war, the Americans arrived, and they continued to arrive until their numbers reached into the millions. U.S. forces would tip the balance on the battlefield. The war would be won by them and their weary Allies. An armistice was signed on November 11, 1918, with peace negotiations scheduled for early 1919. And now their leader, the President of the United States, was on his way to Paris, the first U.S. president to sail to Europe during his time in office.

A U.S. Army artillery crew fires at German forces at Saint-Mihiel, France, in September 1918. A U.S. victory here helped stop the Central Powers' move toward Paris.

As Wilson rode along the streets of New York the crowds cheered him on, all the way to the harbor, where an army transport ship, the *George Washington,* was docked, waiting to take him across the Atlantic to the peace talks outside Paris. Amid the din of sirens and horns, Wilson strode up the gangplank and the great military ship slipped out into the harbor, past the Statue of Liberty, as airplanes and great zeppelins, built in Germany before the war, dotted the skies.

A MAN WITH A PLAN

Wilson had entered the European conflict with great reluctance. He understood the sacrifices the American people would have to make, especially the young boys who would fight for their country on foreign soil. But he had gone into the war with the intention of helping to reshape the postwar world. He imagined a world where war was no longer an option, or at least would be a last resort. He believed the war, should the Allies win, would not only serve to rescue western civilization, but would help spread the seeds of democracy across the European continent and, perhaps, around the world.

For too long, he thought, empires had controlled too many peoples in Europe. The German Reich, the Austro-Hungarian Empire, the Turks and their ancient Ottoman Empire, even Czarist Russia, which had fought initially alongside the Allies, then dropped out of the war—these states had restricted the lives of millions of subject peoples, including the Poles, Lithuanians, Latvians, Estonians, Arabs, Czechs, Slovaks, and South Slavs. Many of these downtrodden peoples knew of Wilson and his plan for their futures. The president's proposal for peace in Europe, called his 14 Points, had been translated into all their languages on leaflets and dropped by planes. They filtered down to earth, promising freedom and nationalism. Imperial subjects now longed for the day that Wilson's plan might reach them. If only he could provide a new direction for his European counterparts; if only he could help bring down empires and establish democracy; perhaps then, the sacrifices of his countrymen might prove crucial in those early years of the twentieth century.

A HERO'S WELCOME

When his ship reached Europe Wilson was more hopeful than ever. Everywhere he was greeted by the same scene, so similar to the send off he had experienced in New York City. When he landed in the French port of Brest he was greeted by huge banners reading "Hail the Champion of the Rights of Man" and "Honor to the Founder of the Society of Nations." In the streets of Paris more banners—"Wilson the Just"—greeted him. As his horse-drawn carriage traveled along the French boulevards, the shouts of countless thousands of Parisians, tears of joy streaming down their faces, rang in his ears; cries of accolades to the President, endlessly shouting his name: "Vilson! Vilson! Vilson!"

The crowd in Paris was almost uncontrollable. Some people had paid as much as 300 francs for a place along the parade route. Three entire divisions of French soldiers had been assigned to the route, just to protect the President from the teeming throng of people. As great cannon were fired, the first since the last day of fighting two months earlier, Wilson waved his hand and tipped his top hat. Girls and women showered his carriage with flowers until he was nearly covered in them.

Sensing the Mood

As he continued his European tour prior to the opening of the Versailles Conference, Wilson was repeatedly welcomed with endless shouts of enthusiasm. They cheered him in England, then in Italy. For the parade in Rome the streets were sprinkled with golden sand, a tribute dating back to the days of the Roman Caesars, when successful generals were granted triumphal marches through the city. More banners sang the praises of the U.S. president: "Welcome to the God of Peace." In the city of Milan the mass of people bordered on the hysterical. Newspapers referred to Wilson in terms fitting a world conqueror: "The Savior of Humanity," "The Moses from Across the Atlantic."

None of it was lost on Wilson. He soaked it all in, considered its meaning, and believed he understood that the enthusiasm was not just for him, but in anticipation of the future. In London, speaking to a large crowd at the city's Guildhall, he interpreted the emotions of the people who had greeted him by the tens of thousands, as historian H. W. Brands notes:

> I do not believe that it was fancy on my part that I heard in the voice of welcome uttered in the streets of this great city and in the streets of Paris something more than a personal welcome. It seemed to me that I heard the voice of one people speaking to another people… As I have conversed with the soldiers, I have been more and more aware that they fought… to do away with an old order and to establish a new one.

Wilson went on, addressing what he believed that "new order" would be based on, that it would become "a single overwhelming, powerful group of nations who shall be the trustee of the peace of the world."

All this was just what Wilson wanted. Among his 14 Points, his plan for the world's future, the president had included an international body unlike any other the world had ever seen. His "League of Nations" would bring countries from every continent into one great forum, where issues could be discussed and war relegated to the scrap heap.

When the conference for peace opened at Versailles on January 1, 1919, Wilson would soon discover whether his plan for peace would become reality. Would his fellow allies support his 14 Points? Was the world poised to enter a completely new phase, with national leaders ready to reveal a united front and join together in a forum of mutual interests? Would the world become "safe for democracy"? What of Wilson's League? What of Europe's future? Which way were the winds of international change going to blow?

The Impact of Immigration by the 1920s

By 1914, millions of immigrants from Southern and Eastern Europe were flooding into the United States. By 1928, together with early immigrants, they formed a significant part of populations in cities across America. This led to social unrest and the introduction of laws limiting new immigration.

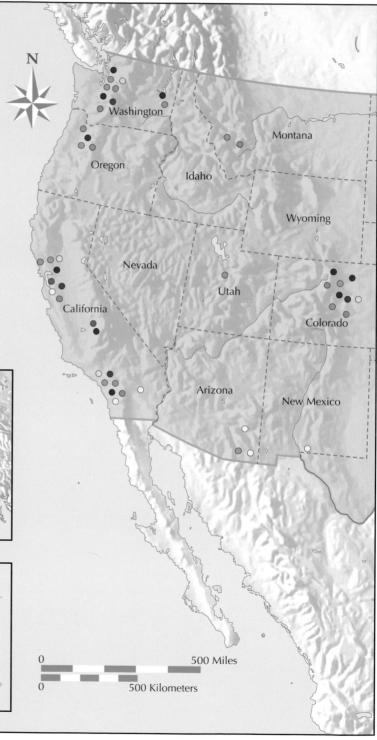

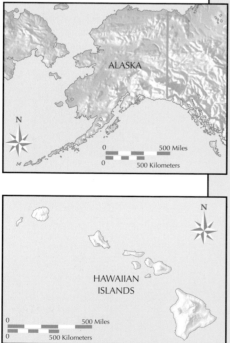

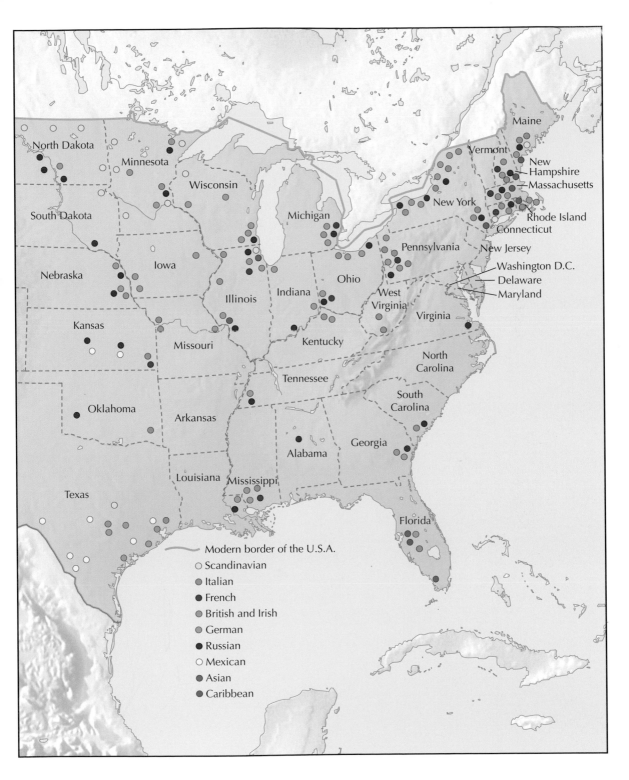

North Dakota

Minnesota

Wisconsin

South Dakota

Michigan

Maine

Vermont

New
Hampshire

Massachusetts

New York

Rhode Island

Connecticut

New Jersey

Pennsylvania

Washington D.C.

Delaware

Maryland

Nebraska

Iowa

Illinois

Indiana

Ohio

West
Virginia

Virginia

Kansas

Missouri

Kentucky

North
Carolina

Tennessee

Oklahoma

Arkansas

South
Carolina

Georgia

Alabama

Louisiana

Mississippi

Texas

Florida

Modern border of the U.S.A.

○ Scandinavian

● Italian

● French

● British and Irish

● German

● Russian

○ Mexican

● Asian

● Caribbean

15

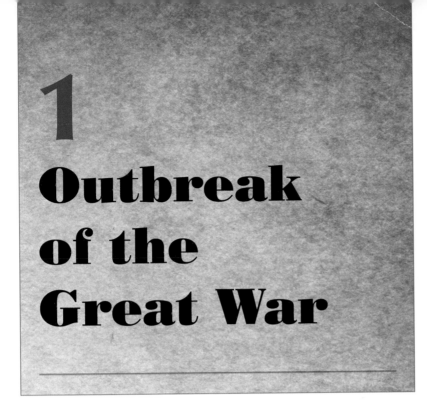

1

Outbreak of the Great War

As Woodrow Wilson prepared to assume the presidency in March 1913, he came to the office with little background or experience in foreign affairs. Earlier in his life he had served as a college professor, and became well-known and popular for his public speaking engagements. He had risen to president of Princeton and served eventually as a progressive governor of New Jersey. Wilson's background had prepared him for public service and the carrying out of domestic policy. It is not surprising, then, that he said just prior to taking office as the nation's chief executive, notes historian James Chace, that it "would be an irony of fate if my administration had to deal chiefly with foreign affairs."

THE CHALLENGE OF WAR IN EUROPE

That particular irony caught up with Wilson early in his first term as president. Events unfolding in Latin America and Europe preoccupied him almost immediately. The Mexican

Revolution presented problems right at America's backdoor. But no foreign policy issues challenged him, or the entire nation, more than the war that broke out in Europe in the summer of 1914. That war would tear apart the fabric of the entire European continent and beyond. It would devastate whole national landscapes and ultimately destroy nearly an entire generation of young European men.

When it began that fateful summer, the war represented the first generalized conflict to engulf Europe in nearly a century. The last time Europeans had fought a broad-based war was during the later 1790s through to 1815, when the Napoleonic Wars saw action from the North Sea to Russia and the Middle East to the Iberian Peninsula. But, with an established balance of power in place following Napoleon Bonaparte's defeat and exile from France in 1815, the continent then witnessed 99 years of widespread peace, with only a few small-scale conflicts in between. The Crimean War of the 1850s and the Franco–Prussian War of 1871 were tiny affairs overall, having little significant impact on the geopolitics of the nineteenth century. Europe experienced great change between 1815 and 1914, while steering clear of full-scale conflict.

Causes of War

However, the decades leading up to the outbreak of the Great War were years in which, it sometimes seemed, the powers of Europe engaged in activities that could only lead eventually to wholesale war. The Industrial Revolution, for example, which had begun in the eighteenth century, had now resulted in the creation of new weapons systems, including airplanes, early tanks, submarines, battleships, poison gas, and the machine gun. Then the European powers had competed with one another in the establishing of colonies around the world, primarily in Asia and Africa. That scramble for colonies had put nations that had not shared a border in Europe next door to one another on other continents. And in the decades before the war the nations of Europe had been forming interlocking treaties, by which they agreed to ally themselves to one another in time of war. Two great alliances had been formed: those nations that became the Triple Alliance—Germany, Austria-Hungary, and Italy—and the Triple Entente, led by Great Britain, France, and Russia.

The Assassination of Archduke Franz Ferdinand

Several of the important European nation states—Germany, Austria-Hungary, Britain, Russia—also controlled empires. As imperial powers, these states sometimes had control over other nations and regions whose people sought to gain their freedom or independence. In some of those controlled states, nationalistic movements had sprung up in opposition to their colonial oppressors. That nationalism would lead a band of Serbian conspirators, members of a terrorist organization known as the Black Hand, to plot the assassination of the heir to the Austro-Hungarian throne, Archduke Franz Ferdinand, in June 1914.

The archduke's murder took place in the city of Sarajevo, capital of the Balkan state of Bosnia, which was then under Austrian control. Gavrilo Princip, a 19-year-old member of the Black Hand, succeeded in shooting the archduke and his wife, Sophia, in their touring car as they prepared to leave the city. As for Franz Ferdinand and his wife, the day of their deaths was their wedding anniversary.

The assassination started a chain of events that soon plunged Europe into full-scale war. Austria declared war on the Balkan state of Serbia, the home of the members of the Black Hand, and a nation surrounded by territories of the Austro-Hungarian empire. This led the Russian government to deliver a warning to the Austrians not to attack Serbia, since the Russians were allied to it. With the threat of Russian mobilization in the wind, the German government—linked to Austria through the Triple Alliance—mobilized instead and sent troops toward France, as military contingency plans dictated. On the way, the Germans had to pass through Belgium. When they requested permission from the king of Belgium to march through his country, Leopold denied the Germans, stating that "Belgium is a nation, not a road." The Germans marched through anyway.

With France now under attack, the Triple Entente led Great Britain to declare war on Germany. The house of cards was toppling dramatically. By August 1914 all the major powers of Europe were at war. The exception was Italy, which did not live up to its treaty obligations to Germany and Austria. In 1915 Italy did join the war effort, but only after switching allegiances, entering the conflict on the side of the Allies.

A DECLARATION OF NEUTRALITY

At the outset of the war the United States watched the conflict unfold, uncertain of the future. Many Americans could not imagine the need for U.S. involvement in the rapidly expanding war. A writer for one U.S. publication, *The Literary Digest,* wrote, notes historian George Tindall: "Our isolated position and freedom from entangling alliances inspire our press with cheering assurance that we are in no peril of being drawn into the European quarrel." As for President Woodrow Wilson, he immediately declared the United States should remain neutral, as he said, "in thought as well as in action."

Yet the President's admonition was not that easy for significant numbers of Americans. At that time approximately one-third of Americans—more than 32 million out of a population of 92 million—were either foreign-born or the children of at least one parent who was foreign-born. With 8 million Germans in America, 4 million Irish (who generally hated the British), as well as Italians, Russian Jews, and millions of others from a host of European countries, being impartial did not come easy. Taking sides, at least in spirit, was likely more normal among Americans than staying neutral. Even Wilson, who was a great admirer of the British, found neutrality difficult.

Over the next nearly three years the United States government maintained its neutral stance. In 1915 two of the most popular songs in America were "Don't Take My Darling Boy Away" and "I Didn't Raise My Boy to Be a Soldier." But, during those same years, a series of factors gradually, but inevitably, pushed the United States closer and closer to taking sides with the Allies, as well as a direct involvement in the conflict.

SUBMARINE WARFARE

One significant factor leading the United States into the war was Germany's repeated practice of violating America's rights as a neutral country. Early in the war Great Britain violated U.S. neutrality by declaring the North Sea a military zone and banning all neutral ships from those waters unless they first passed inspection in a British port. Americans protested the move, and Wilson condemned the practice. The policy was irritating, but not one destined to cause the United States to go to war against the British.

The real violator of U.S. neutral rights proved to be Germany. The Germans had built several submarines prior to the war, knowing their navy would be unable to match the British navy ship for ship. They relied on these subs—known to the German navy as "Underwater Boats" or "U-Boats," from the German *Unterseeboot*—to prowl the waters around Great Britain, as a counter to the British naval blockade of the

European continent. The German government announced that any ships discovered in the waters around Great Britain would be fired on without warning. The German practice soon became "unrestricted submarine warfare." Nothing in the water was off limits to German submarines, including merchant vessels and large passenger liners, which often carried more than 1,000 people onboard.

The Sinking of the *Lusitania*

President Wilson responded by condemning the German declaration as a violation of America's neutral rights on the high seas, but to no avail. In late March, a British steamer was sunk in the Irish Sea, with one American drowned. In early May, a U.S. tanker was sunk, with the loss of two lives. Then, on May 7, 1915, a German U-Boat sank a British passenger liner, the *Lusitania*, within sight of the Irish coast. Nearly 1,200 people were killed as the unarmed liner sank in just 18 minutes. Among the dead were 128 Americans.

The American people were immediately outraged. Former president Theodore Roosevelt called the sinking of the *Lusitania* an act of piracy. Wilson, highly concerned, but not prepared to go to war, took the moral high ground, notes historian Tindall: "There is such a thing as a man being too proud to fight," he said, before adding: "There is such a thing as a nation being so right that it does not need to convince others by force that it is right."

Less than a week following the attack, Wilson's secretary of state, three-time presidential candidate William Jennings Bryan, issued a demand that Germany halt its unrestricted submarine warfare. The German government replied that the *Lusitania* had been armed and had been carrying a cargo of weapons and ammunition. (The first claim was false, the second true.) With Germany unyielding, Wilson ordered Bryan to issue another ultimatum by early June. Fearful of pushing

The *Lusitania* sails from New York for England on
May 1, 1915. On April 22, the German Embassy in
Washington D.C. had issued a warning that the
Atlantic Ocean was a war zone. The ship was sunk by
a German U-Boat off the coast of Ireland on May 7.

Germany to the brink of war with the United States, Bryan refused, choosing instead to resign his post. A new secretary of state, Robert Lansing, issued the second ultimatum.

The *Arabic* Pledge

Behind the scenes the Germans did issue an order to their submarine commanders to avoid hitting passenger liners. Yet on August 19 another British liner, the *Arabic*, was sunk by a German submarine while steaming across the Atlantic toward New York City, killing 45 people, including three Americans. With Americans up in arms, the German ambassador, Count Johann H. von Bernstorff, secured from his government in Berlin a promise, which he made public on September 1, 1915. The Germans pledged to announce their intentions before attacking civilian vessels, such as passenger liners, and provide a 30-minute window to allow passengers and crew members to be removed from the ship to safety. This "*Arabic* Pledge" managed to defuse the situation, at least for the moment.

ECONOMIC AND CULTURAL TIES

There were additional reasons why Americans found neutrality difficult during the early years of the war, including strong economic ties with several Allied nations, especially Great Britain. Prior to the war, the United States had traded more with the British than any other nation in Europe and the war only upped that level of trade, including the shipment of arms and other war materials. Weapons and ammunition became big business between U.S. companies and the Allies. Between 1914 and 1916 Allied purchases of U.S. goods increased four-fold. In 1914, U.S. companies shipped $6 million in munitions to the Allied powers, but the figure skyrocketed to $500 million in arms deliveries, largely ammunition, by 1916.

Not only was the United States deeply connected to Great Britain through trade, but the two countries shared long-standing historical and cultural ties. Most Americans were sympathetic toward the British concerning the war, as Wilson himself was. The President was a longtime admirer of British literature, culture, and politics. He believed strongly in the parliamentary form of government. By contrast, Germany and the United States did not have a shared history to any extent. Germany, in the eyes of many Americans, had changed during the previous 40 years, since the formation of the German Empire in 1871. It had become increasingly militaristic and even menacing, which did not draw many Americans to support the Kaiser and his countrymen. Thus three factors—violations of America's neutral rights on the high seas, economic connections with the Allies, and historical and cultural ties with Great Britain—drew large numbers of American citizens to support the Allies, despite Wilson's earlier calls for neutrality.

A REVERSAL IN GERMAN POLICY

Despite announcing the "*Arabic* Pledge," just seven months later the Germans broke their promise with the unannounced sinking of a French passenger liner, the *Sussex,* on March 24, 1916, resulting in the deaths of four Americans. Wilson immediately threatened to break off diplomatic relations between the United States and Germany, prompting a response by the German government in the form of the "*Sussex* Pledge." A variation on the previous policy of limited submarine warfare, the new German promise was to issue a warning before sinking liners, in order to provide for the safety of the passengers and crew.

Wilson was slightly optimistic, but just three months later a wary U.S. Congress cautiously passed the National Defense Act, which called for a near doubling of the regular army from 90,000 to 175,000 troops and a later enlargement to 223,000 men. It also established a National Guard of 440,000 troops. Congress then passed the Naval Construction Act in August, which authorized spending up to $600 million on a three-year naval expansion program.

That fall the President retained his office during the election, defeating Republican challenger Justice Charles Evans Hughes, a former Progressive New York governor and more recently a member of the U.S. Supreme Court. The Democrat Party hammered out a platform of positions that endorsed Progressive social legislation, as well as holding the line for neutrality, while calling for national preparedness in case the war engulfed the country. The slogan "He Kept Us Out of War," a reminder of Wilson's sometimes deft maneuvering over the previous two years, rang clear to many Americans. The election was fairly close, with Wilson taking 277 electoral votes to Hughes' 254, while the popular vote stood at 9 million votes for Wilson and 8.5 million for Hughes. Wilson captured many Progressive votes, which in the 1912 election had gone to Roosevelt and the Bull Moose Party.

Deal or No Deal?

No sooner was Wilson reelected than he made overtures for peace between the Allied and Central Powers. His call seemed to elicit a positive response from Germany, with the Kaiser's government agreeing to meet at a neutral site. Only then would the Germans reveal their stipulations for peace. The Allied Powers had already made it clear that they intended to assess war damages, or reparations, against Germany at any future peace talks. Still, Wilson was hopeful. Only after he spoke to the Senate, where he suggested the United States had a right to participate actively in helping establish a lasting peace after the conclusion of the war, were Germany's true intentions revealed—the return to unrestricted submarine warfare. The public announcement was made on January 31, 1917, effective the following day. The possibility of peace talks vanished, and every Allied sea vessel was again a target. A report in a New York newspaper, *Brooklyn Eagle,* notes historian Tindall, observed that "Freedom of the seas will now be enjoyed by icebergs and fish."

A PATH TO WAR

The German government's announcement that they would resume unrestricted submarine warfare disappointed and upset Wilson deeply. Wilson's close advisor and friend, Edward House, observed, notes historian H. W. Brands: "The President was sad and depressed, and I did not succeed at any time during the day in lifting him into a better frame of mind." Wilson had held high hopes for his peace initiative, but the Germans had suddenly dashed those possibilities to the ground.

The president then realized he had no real choice but to cut off diplomatic relations with Germany. To that end he called a joint session of Congress on February 3 and delivered a speech, stating: "This Government has no alternative consistent with the dignity and honor of the United States." Yet he remained cautious. War might still be avoided. "We do not desire any hostile conflict with the Imperial German Government," assured Wilson. "We are the sincere friends of the German people… We shall not believe that they are hostile to us unless and until we are obliged to believe it."

The Zimmermann Note

Despite Wilson's words, the German government further played its hand over the weeks that followed, widening the gap of trust between itself and the United States. Early in February 1917 British naval intelligence agents intercepted and decoded a secret telegram sent by the German foreign minister, Arthur Zimmermann, to the German embassy in Mexico City. The cable suggested to the Mexican government that an alliance be established between the two countries and Japan (which was then fighting in the war as an ally of Great Britain and France) against the United States. This was in case the United States entered the war at some later date. The offer to the Mexicans made some sense, since Wilson had recently sent U.S. forces into Mexico and did not have the trust and friendship of the Mexican government. To entice the Mexicans into an alliance, the communiqué suggested that Germany would help Mexico to recover all the territory she had lost during the Mexican–American War of 1846–48, described in the telegram as "the lost territory in Texas, New Mexico, and Arizona." (Never mind that Texas had fought for its independence from Mexico a decade before the Mexican War.)

This suggestion could not have blown up more intensely in the face of the German government. The Mexican government, still struggling with the continuing revolution and other domestic problems, was little interested in going to war on the side of the Germans. Nor, for that matter, were the Japanese tempted by the crazy suggestion. The most overt response was on the part of the U.S. government.

Congress Gives Its Support

The cable message was routed to President Wilson, who then had a decision to make about its contents. He could keep the intercepted message a secret from the American people, whom he knew would be outraged by the suggested alliance, or he could make it public, knowing that it might lead directly to U.S. involvement in the war. He chose to publicize the message, handing its contents over to the Associated Press. The revelation of the German offer to Mexico landed like a bombshell on the U.S. public. Some newspaper editors

A young soldier of the 71st Regiment Infantry, New York National Guard, says goodbye to his sweetheart as his regiment leaves for Camp Wadsworth, Spartanburg, S.C., for training to fight in Europe.

splashed headlines that mirrored public sentiment, such as: "Kill the Kaiser!" In the aftermath, Wilson sought permission from Congress to authorize the arming of all U.S. merchant ships. It was not granted, and Wilson was furious.

ON THE EDGE OF WAR

Events then began to speed up, each one seemingly hurtling the United States toward war. In March 1917, revolution broke out in Russia, resulting in the overthrow of the czar, Nicholas II. A provisional government was established, but did not remain in power for long, as the revolution continued to unfold and ultimately gave rise to a radicalized government. But in 1917 the provisional government appeared, to such western leaders as President Wilson, a breath of fresh air after the tyrannical rule of the czar. Wilson had long thought that he could not possibly ally the United States with Russia, since the country was a dictatorship. Suddenly Russia became acceptable to Wilson as a potential ally. Russian republican government seemed, for the moment, to be the direction the revolution was taking. Thus, a significant psychological, political, and moral block to America joining the Allies had been removed.

Just a week after the overthrow of the czar, Wilson was further driven toward war when German submarines sank five U.S. merchant vessels, two—the *Illinois* and the *City of Memphis*—on the same day, killing dozens of U.S. citizens.

For a time, Wilson sought any other solution to these international crises and, as some called them, "grave matters of national policy." Secretary of state Lansing wrote, notes historian Brands: "I felt that he was resisting the irresistible logic of events and that he resented being compelled to abandon the neutral position which had been preserved with so much difficulty." Ultimately war seemed the only logical answer.

On March 20 Wilson called a meeting of his cabinet, at which the members agreed unanimously that the President should ask for war. Some even suggested that the choice had, in a way, already been made by the American people. Public opinion certainly favored war. Wilson was not impressed by the observation. "I do not care for popular demand," he said. "I want to do right, whether popular or not." The president left the meeting, stating he would make his decision. Writing later that evening in his diary, Secretary of the Navy Josephus Daniels observed the president as he left his circle of advisors, as historian Brands notes: "President was solemn, very sad!!"

MAKING THE REQUEST

The next day President Wilson requested a joint session of Congress, his purpose plain to nearly everyone. On April 2 he spoke to both Houses, recapping how his administration had, for nearly three years, worked to keep the United States neutral, even as he had tried to bring the warring nations of the world to the peace table. In the meantime the German government had violated U.S. neutral rights by wantonly attacking unarmed, non-military vessels on the high seas. Such flagrant violations of U.S. neutrality could no longer be ignored. Yet even as Wilson asked Congress to declare war on Germany, he was already forming in his mind a picture of the world after the end of hostilities. That picture was most clearly presented in Wilson's words: "The world must be made safe for democracy." Not only was Wilson willing to lead the U.S. people into war to defeat Germany and her allies, but he was prepared to use the outcome of the war as an opportunity to further the spread of freedom around the world. He concluded his speech with stirring words: "It is a fearful thing to lead this great peaceful people into war. But right is more precious than peace."

Congress almost unanimously backed Wilson's request for a declaration of war. The Senate approved the measure on April 4 with a vote of 82 to 6. The House took a little longer to debate the issue and voted for war on the morning of

A CONSISTENT VOICE FOR PEACE

When Congress voted on Wilson's request for a declaration of war against Germany during the first week of April 1917, the vast majority of both houses supported the president's request. In the Senate, only six men voted against going to war, while a little more than one out of eight— 373 to 50—in the House voted the measure down. Among those who voted not to declare war was a new member, a 36-year-old Republican from Montana, Jeannette Rankin. She was the first ever woman in Congress.

Rankin had just been elected to the House of Representatives in 1916, the same year that Wilson was reelected as president. She was known as a suffragist and a social worker, as well as a pacifist who did not support war. When elected, she had spoken about the obligation she felt as one of the few female members of the House. As noted by historian Robert Remini, she observed how

she felt "it was my special duty to express… the point of view of women and to make clear that the women of the country are coming to a full realization of the fact that Congress deals with their problems." Perhaps ironically, Rankin had been elected at a time when women were not free to vote in every state in the Union. The Constitution would not provide for complete women's suffrage until the passage of the Nineteenth Amendment, which, in 1916, was still four years away.

Rankin never wavered from her core belief in pacifism. In 1941, when President Franklin Roosevelt requested a declaration of war from Congress against the empire of Japan, which had attacked U.S. naval and air forces in Hawaii, Jeannette Rankin again voted against going to war. In fact, she was the only member of both houses of Congress to not vote favorably for war.

April 6, the tally standing at 373 to 50. At precisely 1:18 that afternoon, President Wilson signed the resolution.

Some senators and congressmen questioned whether his call to spread democracy was a bit idealistic. Wilson had, after all, called on the American people to embark on a great crusade, a "war to end all wars." Some were uncertain of Wilson's capacity to lead the nation as commander in chief. He had never served in the military, having chosen not to serve in the Spanish–American War. He had spent an academic career studying politics, but not the art of war. He was almost by nature and religion reluctant to go to war. But the die was now cast. The war that had been fought for years on battlefields so far removed from the United States had finally arrived on America's doorstep.

2

The War at Home

As soon as Congress declared war on Germany, the United States began to gear up for the war effort. But mobilization did not happen overnight. Initial efforts had taken place prior to April 1917 in anticipation of war, but little true progress had been made. Now Wilson and the federal government moved as quickly as possible to mobilize.

MEN IN UNIFORM

On May 18 Congress adopted the Selective Service Act, which established a draft system requiring all males between the ages of 21 and 30 to register for military service. By August 1918 the age bracket had been widened to include those between the ages of 18 and 45. During the entire period of the war, 24 million American men registered with their local draft boards, but only about 11 percent of them (2.8 million men) were actually drafted into the armed services. By war's end, 4.7 million American men had at one time or another served in the U.S. military, but the vast majority of them never reached Europe or any other theater of the war.

Among the troops, 371,000 black Americans served during the war. With segregation being the law of the land, they were typically placed in separate units. Approximately 200,000 black troops were sent to Europe, where nearly all served in non-combatant battalions, even though many of them requested combat assignments. Around 10,000 black men served in the U.S. Navy during the war, again, in such roles as cooks, stewards, and stevedores.

FUNDING THE WAR

Fighting a war on distant soil on such a scale proved expensive. To finance the U.S. effort, Congress authorized the sale of war bonds, which ultimately paid for approximately two-thirds of the war's cost. Such bonds were sold through four Liberty Loan Drives and, at the end of the conflict, a final Victory Loan Drive, which collectively raised $21 billion. These amounts were staggering at the time to most Americans. The entire federal budget for 1916, the year before U.S. involvement in the war, had just hit $1 billion for the first time ever! The remaining war costs were covered through the raising of income tax rates, as well as the levying of excise taxes on such items as railroad tickets, telegraph messages and telephone calls, alcohol, and tobacco. By 1920 the war had cost $33.5 billion—33 times the peacetime federal budget of 1916.

THE WARTIME ECONOMY

With the nation at war, Congress handed sweeping powers to President Wilson. He was given the authority to control domestic industry and production, and to set prices for such common items as food and fuel. He could regulate and even take over businesses such as factories, mines, meat-packing houses, and food-processing facilities, along with all trans-portation systems and communications facilities, such as telegraph and telephone lines.

A sort of Progressivism was applied to the mobilization for war. New agencies were established to regulate specif-ic aspects of the U.S. economy. The War Industries Board (WIB), created in 1917, became a virtual czar over the man-ufacturing sector, empowered to guide production, includ-ing developing new industries needed for the war effort. The WIB regulated business and sought to limit waste and the production of items considered nonessential for the war effort. The National War Labor Board (NWLB) was estab-lished in April 1918 on Wilson's order. The NWLB's purpose

CREATING A GREAT AMERICAN IMAGE

During World War I the U.S. government went to great lengths to "sell" the war to the American people, creating agencies such as the Commission of Public Information (CPI) to spread propaganda through the rallying talks made by the "Four Minute Men," films, and other useful tools. One of the most frequently used methods for steering American thought and action during the war was an artistic campaign—posters.

Artists produced hundreds of full-color posters throughout the war with different goals, but all with the same ultimate intention—to generate

support for the war. Some posters encouraged young men to enlist in the army, navy, or coast guard. Some sought support for the American Red Cross, or other service organizations supporting the war stateside. Others were designed to encourage Americans to purchase war bonds.

Many talented illustrators of the era became involved in producing wartime poster art. One of the most prolific is remembered today for one specific poster. Artist-illustrator James Montgomery Flagg had made his reputation years before the war, largely as a magazine illustrator.

was, generally, to serve as an arbitrator during labor disputes between the owners of factories and other plants and their workers. In the summer of 1918, the War Labor Policies Board was created, again by Wilson, to set wages, worker hours, and working conditions, all on behalf of the effort to mobilize for war.

American Propaganda

To help "sell" the war to the people, the government also established the Commission of Public Information (CPI). This was, for the most part, a propaganda machine, whose purpose was to boost wartime morale, encourage people to support the conflict and buy bonds, and otherwise spin the

Born in Pelham Manor, New York, he took to drawing as a boy and some of his illustrations were published in popular magazines before he reached his teen years. By age 14 he was illustrating for *Life* magazine. By his twenties he was producing illustrations for books, magazines, political cartoons, and advertisements that made him the highest paid illustrator in the United States.

When the war reached America, Flagg used his talent to produce poster art. In all, the New York artist cranked out 45 wartime posters, including his "Wake Up America Day" poster. His most famous poster, still used today in army recruiting stations across the country, portrayed a stern-faced Uncle Sam, dressed in red, white, and blue, facing the viewer with his finger pointing almost accusingly. The caption: "I Want YOU for U.S. Army." During the war, 4 million copies of this poster were produced. When World War II came along, the poster was reissued.

Unknown to many people then and today, James Flagg posed himself as Uncle Sam in this now iconic poster, adding a white goatee to his own face. When asked later why he used himself as the model for the poster, his answer was simple: It saved him the trouble of finding another suitable model.

A World War I recruitment poster encouraging young men to join the Navy . Many recruitment stations used women of the U.S. Naval Reserve to process the enlistment paperwork.

war in a positive way. A total of 75,000 speakers—called "Four Minute Men"—were used by the CPI to go out and talk up the war at local churches, public auditoriums, meeting halls, schools, and theaters. During the war, Hollywood proved a loyal supporter of the U.S. war effort, and Americans could see war films that included titles such as "The Prussian Cur" and "To Hell With the Kaiser."

The CPI was directed by a well-known muckraker named George Creel. He enlisted the writing services of other Progressive reformers, including Ida Tarbell and Ray Stannard Baker, both of whom had written important muckraking pieces before the war. The pens of such writers were put to use creating pro-American propaganda.

"WHEATLESS MONDAY," "MEATLESS TUESDAY"

One crucial piece of the wartime puzzle was food. With the war raging across the continent, many European farming regions were unable to produce both adequate fertilizer to enrich soil and enough food to feed their civilian and military populations. The United States set up a program of food relief to Europe during this period. It was led by Herbert Hoover, at the time an independent mining consultant but later to be the 31st president of the United States. Americans set out to conserve as much food as possible, as well as other natural resources, to contribute to the program.

In late 1917 Congress adopted a proposed amendment to the U.S. Constitution, calling for the prohibition of the manufacture, sale, or transport of alcoholic beverages. While the prohibition amendment (the Eighteenth) had been an earlier goal of the Progressives, it now received further support due to the war. Supporters of the amendment argued that grain should be conserved and made into food, rather than distilled and manufactured into alcohol. The amendment was ratified by the states in 1919 and became the law of the land in January 1920, more than a year after the war was over.

To further conserve food, the government established a voluntary system of setting aside days of the week when certain foods were not to be consumed. The system applied to other resources, as well. There were "wheatless" Mondays and Wednesdays—days when no one was to eat any foods containing grain products. There were "Porkless Saturdays" and "Meatless Tuesdays." To conserve fuel, the government called for "Gasless Sundays," "Heatless Mondays," and "lightless nights." To further limit fuel production, the Fuel Administration introduced daylight saving time, a practice of adjusting clocks in spring and fall still in use today.

OPPONENTS OF THE WAR

From the outset of U.S. involvement in the war, the vast majority of Americans gave it their enthusiastic support. But there were voices of dissent, as well. Determined to keep such voices of opposition to a minimum, Congress passed the Espionage Act in June 1917. The act was intended to punish those who engaged in anti-war activities, including actions considered treasonous and disloyal. In May of the following year Congress beefed up the act with an amendment, called the Sedition Act. This provided stiff penalties of up to $10,000 in fines and 20 years in prison, or both, for any person tried and convicted of disrupting the sale of war bonds, working to limit domestic manufacturing or production, or, notes historian David Kennedy, using "disloyal, profane, scurrilous, or abusive language about the form of government of the United States, or the uniform of the Army or Navy." Throughout the war these acts were enforced by the U.S. Justice Department and some 1,500 people were arrested, leading to 1,000 convictions. Of that number, fewer than 50 received prison terms between 10 and 20 years.

The limiting of U.S. civil liberties under the Espionage and Sedition Acts gave rise to concern in the minds of some Americans. One observer remarked, notes historian George Tindall: "It became criminal to advocate heavier taxation instead of bond issues, to state that conscription was unconstitutional though the Supreme Court had not yet held it valid, to say that the sinking of merchant vessels was legal, to urge that a referendum should have preceded our declaration of war, to say that war was contrary to the teachings of Christ."

Radicals are Silenced

Naturally, these acts hit the more radical element in America quite hard. Various socialist groups were sometimes targeted, such as the radicalized Industrial Workers of the World (IWW), with 100 of its leaders going on trial in Chicago for their opposition to the war. All of the accused were found guilty, crippling the IWW and causing a blow from which the socialist organization was never fully able to recover.

The most famous radical socialist in America, one-time labor organizer Eugene V. Debs, also felt the sting of the acts. Debs had run as the Socialist candidate for president in 1912 and received nearly 1 million votes. He now spoke out against the war, encouraging American men not to serve in the U.S. military. In a speech, he blasted U.S. intervention in the conflict, stating, notes historian Tindall: "I am opposed to every war but one; I am for that war heart and soul, and that is the world-wide revolution." He stated in another speech that he "would a thousand times rather be a free soul in jail than a sycophant and a coward in the streets"—the government was only too happy to oblige him. Arrested under the Espionage Act, Debs was tried and convicted to 20 years in prison. Still, he ran for the presidency again in 1920, from his jail cell, again polling nearly 1 million votes.

Despite challenges to the Espionage and Sedition Acts, the U.S. Supreme Court upheld the acts in the case of *Schenck v. United States*, in 1919. It was in the context of the court's decision that Justice Oliver Wendell Holmes, who had been appointed to the court by President Theodore Roosevelt, made the observation: "Free speech would not protect a man in falsely shouting fire in a theater, and causing a panic." Holmes believed that the actions taken by the accused in the case, a man who had been arrested for distributing anti-draft literature among members of the U.S. military, amounted to "a clear and present danger."

American patriotic sentiment was on display during World War I in street-level ways, as well. U.S. schools banned the teaching of the German language. City orchestras and symphonies refused to perform the music of German composers. Sauerkraut, a traditional German dish, was renamed "Victory Cabbage," and pretzels, another favorite German food, were removed from free lunch counters in many of the nation's saloons and dining halls.

AMERICAN WOMEN PLAY THEIR PART

While the U.S. armed services was a man's world during the Great War, women did make significant contributions to the war effort. They joined service organizations that sponsored bond drives and other war-relief programs. They served in the Red Cross, the Army Nurse Corps, and in the Navy Nurse Corps. But the nature and scope of World War I also presented unique opportunities for American women. As more and more men either enlisted or were drafted into military service, the nation's business and manufacturing sector began to rely on female workers to take the places of their male counterparts.

Women took farming jobs and could be found working in the nation's loading docks and shipyards, as well as in munitions plants, machine shops, mills, and foundries. There were few jobs in America in which women were not employed by the end of the war. Many women who had worked in more traditionally female jobs—stenographers, telephone operators, secretaries, maids and other domestic

U.S. Red Cross nurses serve soldiers at an American Red Cross canteen in France in 1918. The Red Cross is an international, neutral, non-governmental agency that provides humanitarian aid to victims of war.

workers—were suddenly employed in industrial work. One black house servant traded her job for a factory position, saying, notes historian Tindall: "I'll never work in nobody's kitchen but my own any more. No indeed, that's the one thing that makes me stick to this job."

However, the gains made by women in the work force during the war did not generally continue after the conflict was over. Approximately 1 million women served in some form of war-related work, but most of them were young, single women who had been in the work force before the war. The vast majority of them went back to their old jobs after hostilities ceased and their temporary work came to an end. Many women were told that their patriotism should lead them to give up their jobs for the men who would be returning from their war duty.

Some women thought the gains they had made in the work force would continue after the war, but they faced general disappointment. By 1920 there were 8.5 million women working outside the home in America, fewer than the number who had held such jobs a decade earlier. But the contributions of women during the war did lead to one great sea change in America. After years of campaigning for the vote, women gained suffrage in 1920 with the passage of the Nineteenth Amendment. Even Wilson, who had not supported the vote for women before the war, changed his position in support of women's right to vote.

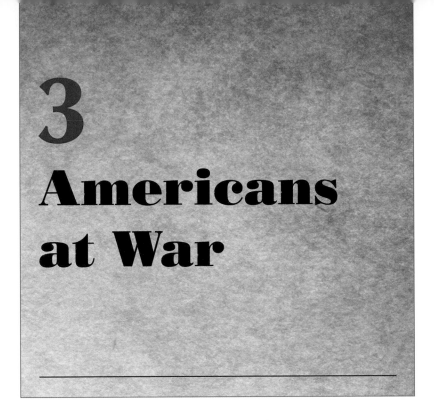

3
Americans at War

Although Congress declared war on Germany, Austria, and the Ottoman Empire in April 1917, American troops, often referred to as "doughboys" on account of dough field rations, engaged in little significant fighting throughout the remainder of the year. Nevertheless, America's declaration of war had come none too soon that spring. The Allies were facing grim prospects on the battlefield.

A NEW KIND OF WAR

The war had turned into a virtual stalemate with trench warfare dominating. Both sides built elaborate trench systems that were protected by barbed wire and the most devastating new weapon of war—the machine gun. The fields lying between each army's defensive lines became known as "no-man's-land." In some places, the Allied and German front-line trenches were separated by only 100 yards (100 meters) of barren ground. Thousands of soldiers died trying to break the stalemate by dashing across this open and deadly ground, only to be struck down by heavy machine gun fire.

Other new weapons had been introduced during the war to break the stalemate. In April 1915 the Germans unleashed a chemical weapon—poisonous chlorine gas. This caused a painful death: The gas liquefied the lungs, causing its

WORLD WAR I EASTERN AND WESTERN FRONTS

The Eastern Front was a line of conflict stretching from the Baltic Sea to the Black Sea through Russia and the Balkans. Its position changed as supremacy ebbed and flowed between the Allies and Central Powers. The Western Front was a series of trenches that ran from the Belgian coast to the Swiss border with France. This line remained constant.

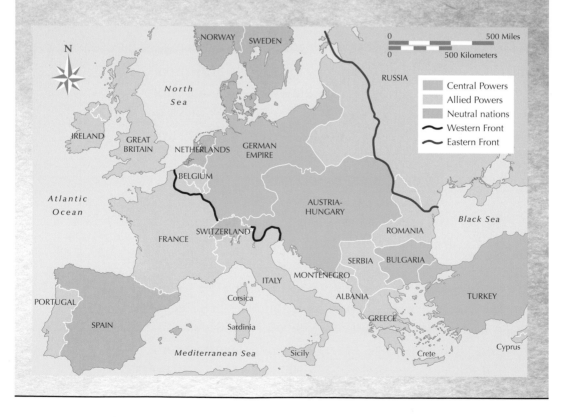

victims to, technically, drown. Great Britain introduced the first tanks to the battlefield in 1916. Airplanes were used during the war for limited bombardment and reconnaissance, and occasionally fought one another in the air in chaotic dogfights. German Zeppelin airships flew over Allied cities, such as London, bombing from the air, and terrorizing the civilian populations.

High Casualty Rates

These new destructive weapons, plus the high concentrations of troops on the battlefields and in the trenches, had caused alarmingly high casualties over the years before the Americans even arrived. In 1916 German troops stormed out of their trenches to attack French positions at Verdun, a struggle that dragged on for six months. When the smoke of war cleared, nearly a million men had fallen in the action, with the French losing 540,000 men, and the Germans 430,000. From July to November 1916 the armies fought a lengthy battle along the Somme River (at which the first tanks were used), resulting in 500,000 casualties for Germany and Allied losses of over 600,000 men. On the first day of battle alone, 57,000 British soldiers fell, most under heavy machine gun fire, and 20,000 of them died.

Eastern and Western Fronts

By early 1917 the Allies were war-weary and uncertain of the war's outcome. The Russians, finding themselves in the midst of a chaotic revolution at home, had dropped out of the war, abandoning the Allies, and suing for a separate peace with the Germans.

In the fall, Germany committed several of its best divisions to fight alongside the Austrians on the Eastern Front and, by October 24, the Austrians and Germans had smashed through Italian lines. By the final weeks of 1917, with the

Russians eliminated from the war and the defeat of the Italians ending the necessity of a serious Eastern Front, the Germans were free to concentrate the lion's share of their forces on the Western Front, its trench lines stretching for

TESTING TO BE A SOLDIER

The Great War proved a brutal testing ground for new weapons of destruction, including machine guns, airplanes, tanks, and poison gas. But another, very different "tool" of war was also introduced in the United States to help prepare men for the various military roles they were expected to fill—psychological testing.

The U.S. Army began using these new types of tests to better assign the right man to the right job. It was an ambitious, perhaps well-intended, program at the time, but untried and probably ultimately flawed. The tests were designed to measure raw intelligence, also called "native" intelligence. But in reality it appears the tests favored those who had more formal education. This led the tests to simply reinforce the racial stereotypes of the day. Whites born in the United States performed the best, achieving the highest scores, while immigrants and minorities, such as blacks, did not score as well.

Ultimately these psychological exams may have served little purpose. The army did not use them extensively and often did not rely on them to determine the assignments given to newly trained recruits. But the tests were used to a great extent in the selection process for officers.

The tests did have a side effect, though. The army's use of psychological tests helped to eliminate much of the American public's doubts about their validity and paved the way for mental testing in peacetime industries and businesses. Following the war, U.S. employers used the tests to screen personnel before making a hire. Colleges began using them as part of the admissions process. Thus, the army pioneered a means of selecting workers and potential college students that remains in place today.

600 miles (965 kilometers) from Belgium across the French countryside like a jagged scar.

THE FIRST U.S. TROOPS ARRIVE

The Americans sent to Europe went under the command of General John J. Pershing, the commander of the American Expeditionary Forces (AEF). Pershing had graduated West Point Military Academy in 1886 and had served in Cuba during the Spanish–American War, in the Philippines, and as commander of the army's expedition into Mexico to capture the *pistolero*, Pancho Villa.

Pershing landed in France early in June 1917, followed before month's end by the first regiments of the U.S. Army's First Division. They numbered only a few thousand men, but they were given a hero's welcome as they marched down the streets of Paris to cheering crowds. By the end of the war 2 million "Yanks" had landed in France, along with equipment vital to the Allied cause, including 17,000 rail freight cars and 40,000 trucks.

However, only small numbers of U.S. troops had reached France even by the early spring of 1918, causing French Premier Georges Clemenceau to appeal to the U.S. high command to speed up the process of delivering U.S. forces to the front. Speaking to an American newspaper reporter, Clemenceau appealed, notes historian Tindall: "A terrible blow is imminent. Tell your Americans to come quickly." But by March 1918, U.S. troops had only been given a stretch of less than 5 miles (8 km) of the Western Front to defend.

Germany Goes on the Offensive

On March 21 the Western Front exploded into full warfare as the Germans launched a heavy campaign, involving 62 of their regiments. The German High Command called the campaign their "Peace Offensive," assuming that they would destroy all Allied resistance, causing the Allies to sue for peace, and giving the Germans the final victory.

Much of the action centered along the Somme River, near Paris. After two weeks of fighting, the Germans had gained large pieces of territory and inflicted huge casualties. There were 250,000 casualties on the British side alone, including the capture of 70,000 British prisoners. German casualties piled up to another 250,000. Over the following two months the Germans reached the Marne River, placing them just 37 miles (60 km) outside Paris.

As for U.S. forces, Pershing had envisioned they would fight in their own units, separately from the Allied armies. Instead, that spring, many U.S. soldiers were fighting alongside British and French troops, used primarily to fill in the gaps within existing Allied armies who were suffering from manpower shortages.

HALTING THE GERMAN ADVANCE

As the fighting continued into the summer of 1918, both sides became desperate to seize a victory, or possibly lose the war. In late May the U.S. Army's First Division managed to capture the French town of Cantigny (kahn-teen-YEE). Their efforts amounted to, according to historian H. P. Willmott, "the first wartime attack of the American Expeditionary Force."

Three days later, on May 31, the U.S. Third Division, in a frenzied last ditch effort less than 40 miles (64 km) outside Paris, fought alongside the French and held off the Germans at Chateau-Thierry. On June 3, the U.S. Third Division blew up a bridge crossing the Marne River, cutting off further German advances, even as they held off the Germans along the Metz Road leading into Paris. On June 6, U.S. forces met the Germans along the Marne, as U.S. Marines led the assault. The fighting was hellish, involving "artillery, gas, mortars, fire from flamethrowers, rifle bullets in sleets," notes historian Gene Smith.

Once the Americans had been thrown full force into the war, they continued to fight with few breaks. Fighting shifted to the Belleau Wood, about 4 miles (6 km) northwest of Chateau-Thierry, involving the U.S. Second Division.

A U.S. Army raiding party weaves between burnt tree stumps and trenches on the Eastern Front in September 1918.

U.S. Pilots Fly Over the Western Front

In 1918 the U.S. Air Service was set up to train and supply aircrew for World War I squadrons in Europe. By the time the war ended, 45 U. S. fighter, bomber, and observational squadrons had served the Allied forces. Among their pilots were Eddie Rickenbacker, later known as the "Ace of Aces," and Quentin Roosevelt, Theodore Roosevelt's youngest son.

A U.S. squadron fighter plane turns to attack a German plane flying over the trenches.

With much-needed support provided by the Fourth Marine Brigade, U.S. forces held off the Germans through six hard days of fighting. Distinguishing themselves above all others in the fighting in Belleau Wood were the U.S. Marines, who advanced under a continuous hail of machine gun fire. Historian Don Lawson describes their gallant efforts:

> As they advanced against this rain of death, the Marines bent forward like men leaning against a hurricane wind… For twenty-four hours a day during the next two weeks the Marines fought their way a savage yard at a time through this nightmare forest. Losses were enormous, yet no thought was given to retreat. On June 26 the following famous message was received by General Pershing: "Entire woods now occupied by United States Marines."

Following the success of the Marines in Belleau Wood, the French government issued an order renaming the forest of such intense fighting as the Wood of the Marines.

SUCCESS AT GREAT COST

In all these battles and others, U.S. forces continued to beat back the Germans for three weeks, a prolonged engagement that cost 5,000 American lives. But the result was a U.S. victory that could only signal to the Germans that the future for them presented few options. The German High Command had thrown its full strength into an offensive that had continued from spring to early summer, and it had failed. The Americans, it seems, had proven that, though inexperienced, they had the ability to fight. (Inexperience plagued even the U.S. staff officers, who administered from behind the lines with poor coordination. During the summer of 1918 thousands of U.S. troops were forced to leave their field positions due to a lack of food, and beg rations from other Allied units.)

But the key was the presence of U.S. forces at this point in the war. And their numbers were increasing rapidly. In May 1918, U.S. forces along the Western Front numbered approximately 500,000 men. By mid-July the number had shot upwards to 1 million. Over the next three months even that number had doubled to 2 million. Americans were pouring into the war during its final six months.

A FINAL GERMAN OFFENSIVE

Fighting continued along the front, and, by July 15, the Germans had regrouped and poured all they had into one more ferocious offensive—their fifth of the war—this time near the French city of Reims. The German strategy was to attack on either side of Reims, then cross the Marne, where Allied forces would become pinned down, while the Germans then launched another front far to the north in Flanders. But the German offensive was no sooner launched than their advance ground to a near halt by the evening of July 16. The German advance was hampered by high rates of desertion and spreading outbreaks of influenza. The Allies had prepared well before the offensive began, and the Germans were, notes historian Willmott, simply "out-thought and out-fought both strategically and tactically."

By July 18, Field Marshall Ferdinand Foch ordered a counterattack, with the First and Second U.S. Infantry Divisions, alongside the First French Moroccan Division, spearheading the assault. The German army melted away, overwhelmed, and the war had reached its tipping point. The tide of conflict had finally turned in the Allies' favor.

THE BATTLE OF THE ARGONNE FOREST

Along the Western Front, the Allies now took the offensive. During the fighting that July, U.S. forces fought as a separate army under Pershing's command. A half million American doughboys, reinforced by French troops and with British planes flying overhead, launched a full-force assault in the region surrounding the town of St. Mihiel. After several days of fighting this region fell under the control of the U.S. military.

The doughboys continued to advance, against heavy artillery and machine gun fire, heading for Sedan, a highly fortified and strategic stronghold that the Germans had held since 1914. For 47 days, U.S. troops pushed forward, the fighting reaching epic levels. From September 26 through October 3 the Americans kept the Germans on the defensive, relentlessly pushing them back. On October 4, General Pershing sent in fresh forces, many of whom were already hardened combat veterans.

Death and disease stalked the Americans. By October 5, 16,000 of Pershing's men had been struck down, not by bullets, but by the flu. Still, they fought on. Throughout these weeks of fighting, Americans suffered 120,000 casualties, including 26,000 men killed. Thousands of tons of artillery shells were fired by U.S. gunners into German lines in the Argonne Forest—more, in fact, than the Union Army used during the entire Civil War.

Tenacity was the order of the day. The Germans only retreated out of "the forest a tree at a time and individual deeds of heroism were being performed hourly," notes historian Lawson. By mid-October Pershing's army had advanced over territory formerly held by the Germans along an offensive line more than 100 miles (160 km) long, placing Pershing in command of nearly one-quarter of the entire Allied concentrated front. He did not remain behind the lines, but visited the front several times to speak to his weary, exhausted men, notes historian David Trask: "Men, if you can stick this out a little longer I'll have you out of here in a few weeks."

Pershing's men fought on, certain that victory was within their grasp. By early November his advance units had broken the last point of German defense, the Hindenburg Line. Less than a week later the German high command made overtures for an armistice. The following day, November 7, the German leader, Kaiser Wilhelm II, abdicated his throne and fled to exile in the Netherlands. On November 11 an armistice was signed at 11 A.M., ending the fighting of World War I. That evening Pershing's jubilant staff held a party, dancing to records on a rickety Victrola. Even Pershing danced.

VICTORY FOR THE ALLIES

The Americans had tipped the scales of war in favor of the Allies. U.S. forces had slogged across France under the stern leadership of General Pershing, and matched and bested all the German military could offer. Of that final battle, Pershing wrote:

> Between September 26th and November 11th, 22 American and 6 French divisions, with an approximate fighting strength of 500,000 men… had engaged and decisively beaten 43 different German divisions, with an estimated fighting strength of 470,000. Of the 22 American divisions, four had at different times during this period been in action on fronts other than our own. The enemy suffered an estimated loss of over 100,000 casualties in this battle and the First Army about 117,000. It captured 26,000 prisoners, 874 cannon, 3,000 machine guns, and large quantities of material.

By the end of the battle, which delivered an end to the war, Pershing had commanded 1.2 million troops and had brought about the greatest military victory in U.S. history to that date.

4

A Hard Fought Peace

When President Wilson went to Congress to call for a declaration of war against Germany in April 1917, he did so with resolve, yet with reluctance. He had worked for more than two years to steer the United States clear of direct military involvement in Europe's ever-expanding conflict and to keep America at peace. However, Germany's actions against the United States, especially its practice of unrestricted submarine warfare, had pushed the president, who took the issue of international law seriously, until he had no choice but to respond with military action of his own. He did not like going to war even then. He told an aide, notes historian George Tindall: "I have this war, and the only thing I care about on earth is the peace I am going to make at the end of it." It was this more than anything else—to help redirect the world away from future wars—that motivated President Wilson to throw America's military might into the worldwide fray.

Yet just how Wilson would steer and even direct the European powers, who had already lost so many hundreds of thousands of soldiers and who had witnessed the war unfold on their own soil, was a question in itself. Historian John Whiteclay Chambers notes how the Progressive writer Randolph Bourne doubted Wilson's ability to set the future course for the world after the war. Bourne wrote: "If the war is too strong for you to prevent, how is it going to be weak enough for you to control and mould to your liberal purposes?"

American soldiers of Company M, 6th Infantry Regiment, celebrate the World War I armistice at Remoiville, France, on November 11, 1918. It would be many weeks before the troops returned home.

WILSON'S PLAN FOR PEACE

Wilson unveiled his plan for peace after the war long before the conflict was over or even decided. On January 8, 1918, the President stood before Congress and presented his plan, stating that his was "the only possible program for world peace." It was a comprehensive collection of proposals, soon dubbed as Wilson's 14 Points, or principles.

The first few points in the plan set the direction for western civilization after the end of the war. Wilson believed that several factors before the opening of hostilities in the summer of 1914 had caused the war in the first place. Logically, eliminate those "causes" for war, and future wars could be avoided. He isolated five reasons for the Great War, which paralleled Points 1 through 5.

First, Wilson called for an end to secret diplomacy. Prior to the war, European powers had entered into military agreements secretly, making it difficult for one nation to know exactly which other powers it might have to contend when it went to war with only one country. Wilson had a point. His second suggestion was to promote and support freedom of the seas, rather than have them controlled by the nations with the most powerful navies. Wilson certainly had Germany's practice of unrestricted submarine warfare in mind here. Three, Wilson suggested the removal of all trade barriers and restrictive tariffs. These had caused economic rivalries between the world's powers that had led to war.

His fourth proposal was for arms reduction. Prior to the war, European powers and other nations, such as Japan, had built up massive military machines that bristled with modern weaponry, including battleships, airplanes, and immense artillery pieces. If the advanced nations reduced their militaries on a ratio basis, the balance of power would remain the same, but the means of warfare would be lessened in number. His fifth proposal was designed to reduce tensions and competition over colonies by establishing temporary international control of the various European-held colonies around the world, replacing the imperialism that had led European leaders to set up those colonies in the first place.

Empires and Borders

Nearly all of Wilson's remaining points in his postwar blueprint focused on the liberation of various nation states in Europe from imperial control and the reestablishment of previous national borders. Concerning the latter, Wilson called for enemy armies of occupation to be removed from Russia, Belgium, France, and Italy and for a recreated Poland. Four European empires had been brought down by the war—Czarist Russia, Germany's Second Reich (or Empire), the Austro-Hungarian Empire, and the Ottoman Empire, held by the Turks. Each empire had exerted control over various European peoples. The stage had been set by the Allies' victory over those empires to now free former subject peoples and, in some cases, reestablish their old states or create completely new ones. Wilson's Points 6 through 13 provided the list of affected peoples, including the Poles, Czechs, Slovaks, South Slavs, and others. All these changes reflected Wilson's view of postwar Europe; one in which liberty and autonomy would be the new watchwords.

The 14th Point

As for Wilson's last proposal, his 14th Point, he reserved this for the creation of a "general association of nations"; an international body designed to provide mutual guarantees of national independence and the protection of each nation's sovereignty and territory. This body was destined to become the League of Nations.

Wilson presented his 14 Points to Congress in early 1918. His plan was also presented to the Allied leaders in Europe, then printed in several different languages on leaflets that were dropped by planes over enemy territory as propaganda. With subject peoples aware of the goals of the 14 Points, some stepped up their resistance against Germany and Austria-Hungary. Even some Germans read copies of the 14 Points and saw hope for themselves. Perhaps the Allies might help them receive their freedom once their national leaders were defeated.

THE "BIG FOUR"

On Armistice Day—November 11, 1918—the day designated for the fighting to stop, almost every American celebrated. Schools closed, along with businesses and factories. Church bells rang out the news of the end of the war, as small-town fire engines ran through the streets, their own bells ringing with enthusiasm. Wilson issued a public statement that ran in newspapers across the country. In his words, "Everything for which America fought has been accomplished." At that moment, the words rang true and most Americans believed them, as well. Then, three weeks later, on December 4, 1918, Wilson became the first standing president to leave the United States bound for Europe.

Wilson was given a hero's welcome when he arrived in Paris, with cheering crowds everywhere he went. But when he arrived at the conference at Versailles, his 14 Points met immediate resistance.

The location for the 1919 peace talks was the Palace of Versailles near Paris, built during the reign of the French King Louis XIV. A beehive of meeting rooms, dining halls, and apartments half a mile (800 m) long housed world leaders and their representatives by the hundreds, not just from Europe, but from Africa, Asia, and the Middle East. The conference swiftly became a chaotic series of meetings, at which telephones were in short supply and there were constant difficulties in translating documents into all the languages represented.

Britain, France, and Italy

Three other Allied leaders, along with Wilson, would dominate the peace conference. Even though the U.S. president had been wildly received by throngs of people in Paris, London, and Rome, the leaders of those three nations came to Versailles with their own agendas.

The British Prime Minister, David Lloyd George, had just been elected, having campaigned on slogans that included "Hang the Kaiser" and "Make Germany Pay." He felt he had a mandate from the British people to place the blame for the war on Germany and to assess war damages from her. As to Wilson's point that sought "freedom of the seas," Lloyd George did not intend to surrender Britain's dominance at sea and his nation's naval superiority. The British leader had a greater interest in maintaining and expanding his nation's empire than he did in establishing a League of Nations.

Premier Georges Clemenceau, known as the "tiger" of French politics, intended to crush Germany's remaining power, so that his neighbor to the east would be unable to invade or even menace his country again. As for Italy's Vittorio Orlando, the Italians had entered the war in 1915 with the promise from Great Britain of new territory. He expected just that. Thus, the other three of the "Big Four" did not come to Versailles with Wilson's 14 Points as their own personal blueprint.

COMPROMISE OR QUIT?

Adding to Wilson's frustrations at the Versailles Conference were the secret treaties that nations had already made. Russia had been an ally of Britain and France before dropping out of the conflict in late 1917. The revolutionary Bolshevik leaders, who came to power that year, made public secret treaties that the Allies had made prior to America's entry into the war. The Allies had agreed that Great Britain would take over Germany's colonies, while France, Russia, Serbia, and Italy would annex territory from Germany and Austria-Hungary. In addition, Germany was to pay reparations, or war damages, to the Allied nations after the war. These earlier agreements ran up against Wilson's points about open diplomacy, self-determination for states held by empires, and the end of colonial rule.

Once he realized that these agreements had already been made without his knowledge, Wilson was faced with a dilemma. He would probably not see his 14 Points completely adopted. With no other plan but his on the table, the President saw his immediate options as either walking out of the conference or compromising with his European counterparts, and emerging from Versailles with half a loaf rather than none at all.

At one point Wilson did almost leave the conference in frustration. But he remained because he realized that the future of the League of Nations, and its becoming reality, was entirely dependent on him. It was due to his insistence that discussion of the League was placed at the top of the conference's agenda, and he was appointed chair of the commission set up to write out a charter for the proposed world organization.

On February 14, Wilson and the commission completed their work on the charter. It consisted of 26 articles, the most important reading: "The High Contracting Parties undertake to respect and preserve as against external aggression the territorial integrity and existing political independence of all State members of the League." For Wilson, his work on the commission was always the heart and soul of the Versailles Conference.

OPPOSITION AT EVERY TURN

Not long after completing work on the League of Nations Charter, President Wilson decided to return home to the United States. However, the work of the conference was not completed, and the president made it clear to his colleagues that he would return soon. There was concern on his part that he had been gone from the States for two months, longer than any U.S. president had been out of the country. Returning to America, even temporarily, would also give him an opportunity to speak directly to the American people and talk up his League of Nations.

Upon his arrival back in the United States, Wilson found forces of opposition waiting for him. One of the most outspoken critics of Wilson's proposed League had been former president Theodore Roosevelt. But Roosevelt had died in January. Now the most staunch naysayer was Senator Henry Cabot Lodge of Massachusetts, a longtime friend and political ally of Roosevelt. Like Wilson, Lodge had been a university professor (at Harvard) and held three degrees. He had been known as the "scholar in politics" before Wilson had come along, and the former New Jersey governor had outshone Lodge in his scholarship and his success as a politician.

Those in the Senate who opposed the treaty Wilson brought back from Versailles generally fell into two groups. The "Irreconcilables" were those who were opposed to U.S. membership in the League of Nations, a group that included 14 Republicans and 2 Democrats. As for Lodge, he belonged to the second group, the "Reservationists," who were prepared to compromise with Wilson and rewrite some of the treaty's provisions. However, Wilson would have none of it. He held firm against any changes and, in doing so, ultimately killed the treaty's chances of being ratified by the Senate.

Things were not as simple as Lodge not liking Wilson, however. He did not agree with the president's view of the postwar world. Wilson was an internationalist who believed the United States needed to continue providing leadership for the world community. Lodge was, basically, notes historian H. W. Brands, "an American nationalist."

Once the *George Washington* reached U.S. waters, Wilson set out to speak in support of the League of Nations. He started his campaign in Boston, in Lodge's home state. In an address on February 24, Wilson took a side swipe at Lodge, notes historian Brands: "Any man who resists the present tides that run in the world will find himself thrown upon a shore so high and barren that it will seem as if he had been separated from his human kind forever." As he spoke in other eastern cities, Wilson prompted Lodge to respond. The Massachusetts senator stated that he and his colleagues in the Senate would take a close, discerning look at the League and the entire Versailles Treaty once it was completed. Then he introduced on the Senate floor a resolution that soon received enough support from his fellow Republicans that it passed. The resolution was a statement in opposition to U.S. membership of the proposed League.

Before returning to Paris and Versailles, President Wilson met publicly with former President William Howard Taft, a Republican. The two linked arms together onstage at New York's Metropolitan Opera House, showing the people of the United States that not all Republicans opposed Wilson's work on the treaty and on behalf of the League. Soon after, Wilson again set sail for Europe.

TALKS AND AGREEMENTS

Just as Wilson had faced obstacles back home, he soon met opposition when he stepped back into the great halls of the Palace of Versailles. The work of the conference had continued in his absence and at least two of the Big Four—Clemenceau and Lloyd George—had solidified their positions regarding the treaty. Wilson had left an old friend, Edward House, at the conference to speak for him. During those weeks House had made agreements with the French and British leaders that Wilson did not approve of when he learned of them. This soon led to a falling out between the two old friends. House had undermined the President, and Wilson was left looking as though he had not been in control of his delegation. From that point on the U.S. leader was negotiating from a weakened position.

The other Big Four leaders were not going to take Wilson's idealism about the League of Nations seriously. Lloyd George, for example, intended to get all the reparations out of Germany he possibly could. Historian Brands recalls how the British leader "was on record with talk of hanging the Kaiser and squeezing the German lemon 'till the pips squeak.'" Clemenceau was more determined than ever to reduce Germany's power to nearly zero. Wilson and Clemenceau finally exchanged such heated words that the French premier walked out of one meeting of the Big Four.

THE TREATY OF VERSAILLES

The work on the Treaty of Versailles was not completely finished, with represented nations signing off on the document, until late June 1919. The final draft of the treaty was signed on June 28 in Versailles' Hall of Mirrors. Wilson had, indeed, bargained, often with himself on one side and the other three world leaders on the other. But his compromises finally led to the British and the French accepting the League of Nations.

Redrawing the Map

The treaty did make important changes in the world's geopolitical realities. For one, Germany's colonies were handed off to the Allies, albeit under a mandate system. This meant that the Allied nations did not gain complete control, but were accountable to the colonial administration of the new League of Nations, which would serve as a monitor of sorts.

Territory did change hands and, in several cases, whole peoples gained their independence from colonial rule. The region lying between Germany and France, Alsace-Lorraine, had been a bone of contention between the two powers for years. It was now returned to France. From former German and Russian territory, the nation of Poland was recreated. A completely new country, Czechoslovakia, was formed from

Premier Georges Clemenceau of France (left, with stick), U.S. President Woodrow Wilson (center), and Britain's Prime Minister David Lloyd George (right, hat raised) leave the Palace of Versailles after the signing of the Versailles Peace Treaty on June 28, 1919.

former German and Austrian lands as a homeland for Czechs and Slovaks. For the South Slavs—those formerly living in independent Serbia and other Slavic states controlled by the Austrian Empire—the new nation of Yugoslavia ("land of the South Slavs") was formed.

At some points during the negotiations, the members of the Big Four could have been seen crawling on their hands and trousered knees, poring over large maps, painstakingly redrawing many of the borders of Central and Eastern Europe. In this region, additional nations were liberated from Russia, Germany, and other states—Finland, Estonia, Latvia, and Lithuania. Other countries, such as Italy, Greece, Rumania, and Belgium, had their borders changed.

In addition, the treaty placed the full responsibility for starting the war on Germany. The Allied nations then forced Germany to disarm. War damages were also assessed against Germany. The treaty's "war guilt" clause was a bitter pill for the German people.

THE LEAGUE OF NATIONS

Nevertheless, it was the League of Nations that landed the negotiators at Versailles onto new diplomatic ground. The League headquarters was to be in Geneva, Switzerland, a nation that had not even participated in World War I. The League's structure was fairly simple and included a permanent Secretariat, which was to handle the administration of the organization, and an Assembly, a forum of nations in which every member was represented equally and in which each member country had one vote. While the Assembly was similar to a representative body, the League also included a Council, an executive consisting of five permanent member nations: France, Great Britain, Italy, the United States, and Japan. Other nations were to be included in the Council on a rotating basis. As for Germany, and the newly established

Soviet Union, which had been formed out of the Czar's collapsed Russian Empire, both were excluded from League membership.

The League's Charter, which clearly bore the fingerprints of Woodrow Wilson, did not outlaw or ban war. But each member nation, when joining the League, was to agree that it would make every effort to resolve its issues in a friendly manner and even participate in a "cooling off" period before taking any overt steps toward war. If a member violated these expectations, the other League members had the option of imposing economic sanctions on the aggressor.

Flawed from the Start

Yet, even after months of discussion, argument, and compromise, the League of Nations that emerged from the Versailles negotiations was an imperfect organization. The League Charter referred to nations who might choose to go to war as "aggressors," but the specifics of that term were not clearly defined. The members of the League's executive Council were only empowered to recommend their will to other countries, but had no means of backing up its authority, short of sanctions. Perhaps the most glaring flaw of the League was the system of voting by Council members. Anyone on the Council, whether a permanent or temporary member, held the power of the veto. One vote against a proposal would kill it, since all decisions of the Council had to be unanimous to pass.

There were other weaknesses in the League. The new international organization was supposed to guarantee boundaries between nations, including those that had been drawn up by the Big Four and others at the conference. Some new national boundary lines—especially those of nations such as Czechoslovakia, which were newly established at the conference— had suddenly placed peoples of different nationalities into a new country. For example, the borders of the new Czechoslovakia included some former German territory, the Sudetenland, which was home to 3 million Germans. They had not intended to be manipulated out of their homeland into a new country. Such inadvertent mistakes by the Allied leaders would, within a generation, help lead to the outbreak of World War II.

The League of Nations also suffered from a lack of power to alter the economic policies of either member or non-member nations. While Wilson had included in his 14 Points the elimination of economic barriers such as tariffs, these had not been addressed adequately, and the League had no power to impact such things. Perhaps a final shortfall of the League was that Germany was denied membership, at least until 1926, as was the Soviet Union, which would join the international organization only in 1934. Nevertheless, 60 nations joined the League in a show of support, commitment, and solidarity.

REJECTION BY THE SENATE

As with Germany and the Soviet Union, the United States would not be among their number. By early July 1919, Wilson was back in the United States trumpeting the Versailles Treaty and his League, and hoping for support from the American people. The president even chose to present the treaty in person to the Senate, bringing the document with him to the Senate chamber on July 10, even as heavy rains poured outside. As Wilson walked into the chamber, he was escorted by Senator Lodge, who turned to the president and asked, Wilson's doctor, Cary T. Grayson, later noted: "Mr. President, can I carry the treaty for you?" Wilson's response was emphatic: "Not on your life."

In the Senate Chamber, the president presented the treaty, laying each page out for the gathered senators to read. He then spoke eloquently on behalf of the document that he had worked so hard for over the previous six months. He reminded them that the United States had finally entered the war as the "disinterested champions of right." (With these words, the president was conveniently forgetting that U.S. ships had been sunk by the Germans, which had led the United States into the worldwide conflict.) Wilson spoke of the need for America's "moral leadership" on the postwar world stage. That stage, he continued:

> *… is set, the destiny disclosed. It has come about by no plan of our conceiving, but by the hand of God who led us into this way. We cannot turn back. We can only go forward, with lifted eyes and freshened spirit, to follow the vision. It was of this that we dreamed at our birth. America shall in truth show the way. The light streams upon the path ahead, and nowhere else.*

Despite his well-chosen words, just as Wilson feared, the Senate proved uncooperative. As the chair of the Senate's Committee on Foreign Relations, Senator Henry Cabot Lodge was able to sway his fellow Republicans and reject the League. The Senate did not vote to ratify the Versailles Treaty, either. Oppositional senators were not the only ones in the country who were not in favor of the treaty. Significant numbers of Americans felt the treaty unjustly blamed Germany for the entire war and were opposed to having the United States join the League of Nations, since its members were obligated to carry out and enforce the provisions of that same treaty. Americans noted the article in the treaty that required League members to guarantee the political boundaries of its members. They feared, with justification, that such an obligation might lead the United States into another war in the future.

Wilson's Speaking Tour

When some senators offered their support only if changes were made in the treaty itself, Wilson finally had had enough. He felt he had compromised too much already. After weeks passed without any sign that the Senate would accept the Versailles Treaty or U.S. membership in the League, Wilson turned to an old personal tactic. He would launch a speaking campaign and talk his fellow Americans into pressuring their senators to vote for the treaty.

His speaking tour began in Columbus, Ohio, where a cold drizzle dampened the day, then he was off to Indiana and Missouri, where he was met with larger crowds. He took his talk into the West, visiting Montana and Idaho, then down to California, at each stop pleading to the crowds to give him their support. He warned that U.S. rejection of the treaty and the League of Nations would represent a step backward for civilization and that war would remain the norm. He insisted in Ogden, Utah, that four out of five Americans supported the League of Nations. By failing to support the League, the President insisted during his speech on September 23, "we will serve Germany's purpose." Two days later, in Pueblo, Colorado, he gave one more speech, telling those gathered: "Now that the mists of this great question have cleared away, I believe that men will see the truth, eye to eye, and face to face… There is one thing that the American people always rise to and extend their hand to, and that is the truth of justice and of liberty and of peace."

WILSON IS STRUCK DOWN

The Pueblo speech was his last. Having struggled with high blood pressure for several decades, Wilson experienced a series of incidents during the days following the Pueblo address, until he suffered a debilitating stroke on October 2, one that paralyzed the left side of his body. Wilson had

WOODROW WILSON'S LAST YEARS

For years Wilson had been plagued by health issues. In 1896 he had his first stroke, resulting in the temporary loss of use of his right hand. Twenty years later, a burst blood vessel in his left eye left him temporarily blind. In 1908 he lost the use of his right hand again, at least for a time.

However, the stroke he suffered in the fall of 1919 would prove dire and the results permanent. Through those final 17 months of his term, he had limited mobility and was for a while completely bedfast. His second wife, Edith, whom Wilson had married earlier in his presidency, kept him out of the public eye and even limited official visits by members of Congress and his own cabinet.

In 1921, his presidency at an end, Wilson retired from public service. He had no choice really. With Edith he moved into a house on S Street above Dupont Circle in Washington, so close to the seat of U.S. political power, but relegated by his health to a life of relative obscurity. There were visitors from time to time and his fellow Democrats, led by a young Franklin Roosevelt, established a foundation in Wilson's name, one dedicated to internationalism. But his time as a government figure was over.

Wilson's days passed quietly, with few significant interruptions. He was taken on a daily drive around Washington and loved to attend a local vaudeville theater on Saturday nights. When President Warren G. Harding died in August 1923, Wilson was driven over to the White House for the funeral, but could not muster the strength to get out of the car. Two months later, on November 11, the fifth anniversary of the Armistice, Wilson spoke on the radio, a new medium at the time.

Then, in late January 1924, Wilson was diagnosed by his doctor, Cary Grayson, with stomach failure. The end was near, and the former president knew it. In his memoir, Dr. Grayson recalled Wilson's words: "The machinery is worn out. I am ready." He died on February 3, at his home on S Street. Had Wilson died from his stroke in October 1919, it would have been a martyr's death. More than four years later, his passing seemed an anticlimax.

suffered several strokes throughout the previous 20 years, incidents that had, on different occasions, rendered him temporarily blind and unable to write with his right hand. He had even experienced some sort of "cerebral incident" at the conference the previous April. This time, after six years in the White House and six months at Versailles, the President had been again struck down. He would never completely recover.

The stroke not only brought Wilson down, but also killed any hopes of ratification for the Versailles Treaty by the United States Senate. All hope for U.S. membership in the League of Nations evaporated, as the man who had virtually invented the international organization out of whole cloth could no longer speak on its behalf. Wilson would remain president, serving out his term until the spring of 1921. But his effectiveness had died during those early days in October 1919. He hoped that 1920 might bring another Democrat to the White House, one who could pick up the torch his poor health had forced him to drop. But the election of 1920 ushered in a new era for the United States, as three conservative Republican presidents were to lead America away from the precipice of world leadership and through one of the most unique decades in the nation's history—the Roaring Twenties.

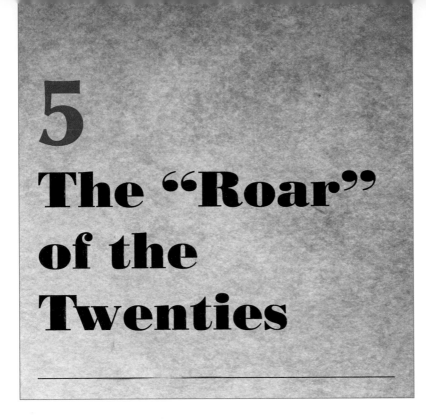

5

The "Roar" of the Twenties

With the end of World War I in November 1918, many Americans were prepared to retreat permanently from the battlefields of Europe, and the Republicans were only too willing to lead them. The war had cost many billions of dollars and delivered significant numbers of casualties—approximately 114,000 U.S. servicemen killed—leaving their countrymen to ponder just what those deaths had accomplished. Although President Wilson was beating the drum of internationalism and a new, greater role for the United States as a leading power in the world, Americans were cautious about joining the League of Nations and being possibly obliged to find another generation of "doughboys" to fight in a future European conflict. Conservative Republicans joined the chorus of caution as they steered the country away from further international responsibility. Let Europe fight its own wars. America needed to keep its nose out of everyone else's business and get on with business of its own—retooling the U.S. economy from wartime production to that of peacetime prosperity.

However, the Senate's rejection of the Versailles Treaty left the U.S. government in an awkward position. Refusal to accept the negotiated agreement officially ending World War I meant that America's war was not technically over. This led Congress to declare the war ended by a joint resolution on May 20, 1920. A debilitated Wilson, nearly restricted to his bedroom in the White House, vetoed the resolution. Things remained in limbo until July 2, 1921, when Congress voted again. With Wilson now out of office, the Congressional move was signed by the new president. Three months later, in mid-October, new and separate peace treaties were signed between the United States and the Central Powers of Germany, Austria, and Hungary.

The last year of his presidency was indeed a difficult one for the incapacitated President Wilson. There was no significant plan to demobilize by bringing the troops home and shifting domestic production. The War Industries Board simply stopped operating on January 1, 1919, and many of the government's contracts for war goods were broken, leaving some industries and businesses in the lurch. Through 1919 U.S. military forces were discharged at the rate of 4,000 a day, which poured men into the U.S. work force at a startling rate.

A NEW, LETHAL ENEMY

Even as the American doughboys were being sent home, the war behind them, a new threat loomed, and one that would cause more casualties than the war itself. In the spring of 1918 a great contagion called the Spanish flu began to spread around the world. It continued for more than a year, ultimately killing more than 22 million victims, a number twice as high as those killed in World War I.

This strong strain of the flu spread across the States quickly due to the number of returning U.S. troops, who brought the disease back with them. Out in Kansas more than 500 soldiers came down with the flu at Fort Riley. Since the flu was a common enough disease, few gave the number serious thought. Then the men began dying in the fort's hospital by the score, revealing that this strain of the flu was,

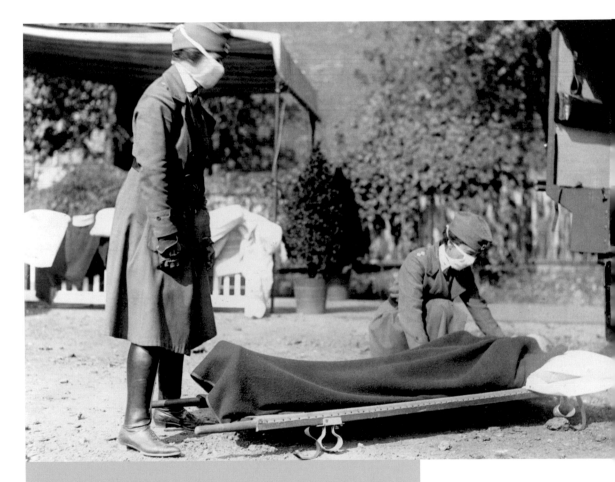

American Red Cross volunteers tend to a patient at an emergency medical station at Washington, D.C., during the influenza epidemic of 1918. In some cities people were required to wear gauze masks in public.

indeed, a killer. Normally, the flu hits hardest in populations of children and elderly individuals, but the Spanish flu killed young adults in large numbers. Throughout 1918, with the war still raging until early November, 43,000 U.S. servicemen died of the Spanish influenza.

In the fall of 1918, U.S. newspaper headlines gave as much attention to the flu as to the final battles of the Great War. In September alone 10,000 Americans died from the disease, with no real treatment available. Everywhere people panicked at the thought of contracting the disease. Millions covered their mouths and noses with handkerchiefs or surgical masks to try to halt the contagion's spread. Public places—theaters, taverns, auditoriums, dance halls—were closed down. Some churches stopped holding public worship services. Fear and the flu reigned in America from September 1918 until early summer of the following year. Then it suddenly ground to a halt, having run through its deadly cycle. During those nine months one in every four Americans had become sick with the flu, and many of them died.

THREAT OF RADICALISM

Americans faced other difficulties in 1919, when race riots exploded that summer across the country. Attacks on black, as well as white, victims led to fights between the races, with killings on both sides. Four days of rioting took place in the nation's capital. But the worst urban violence unfolded in Chicago in late July, when rioting killed 38 and injured more than 500. In all more than two dozen race riots took place in 1919, with hundreds of casualties.

These riots, some inspired by labor strikes, led some people to believe that revolution had spread from Russia to America. Now American radicals, including communists, socialists, and anarchists, called for an uprising of the country's working class. To push their revolution forward, some radicals sent bombs through the U.S. postal system. Forty such bombs were intercepted by postal officials and one managed to reach its target, a Georgia senator who lost his hands unwrapping his deadly delivery. In June the home of the country's Attorney General, Alexander Mitchell Palmer, was destroyed by a bomb. Suddenly, Americans saw the threat of communism coming in through every window, leading the government to engage in a full-scale crackdown.

Raids and Deportations

Attorney General Palmer, who had made his fear of alien immigrants clear to the public, ordered his Justice Department to begin deporting suspected radicalized aliens. He established a new departmental apparatus, the General Intelligence Division, and appointed a young law enforcement agent as its head—J. Edgar Hoover. Hoover, who would one day head another law enforcement agency, the Federal Bureau of Investigation (FBI), began cracking down on radical groups and their members. In November 1919 his division raided the offices of the Union of Russian Workers in a dozen U.S. cities, and many of those arrested were deported immediately, without benefit of a legal hearing.

Two months later, on New Year's Day, more raids were ordered across the country and more than 6,000 suspects were taken into custody, the police usually acting without search warrants. The "Palmer Raids" expected not only to arrest radicals, but to uncover large numbers of bombs and guns. Despite expectations, only three handguns were seized. Nevertheless, the nation continued to call for action. The "Red Menace" seemed so pervasive that even the New York Legislature removed five of its members, each a socialist who had been legally elected. In the U.S. House of Representatives, a newly elected socialist representative from Wisconsin, Victor L. Berger, was denied his seat due to his socialist views, his prior opposition to the war, and the fact that he was of German descent.

Despite Attorney General Palmer's call for a continued and relentless crackdown, America's first real Red Scare had run its course by the summer of 1920. The previous spring Palmer had warned of a great uprising being planned by U.S. Bolsheviks, or communists. Congress and state legislators anxiously responded, calling out state militias and stationing armed guards to protect public buildings and the private homes of congressmen and senators. But when this threatened "May Day Revolt" did not materialize, Palmer only managed to discredit himself. The threat of communist revolution spreading from Russia across the United States played out, as did the bombings in America.

Some in America even began to see more threat in the actions being taken by Palmer and Hoover than in the nation's radicalized element. Even when someone tossed a bomb at the corner of Wall and Broad Streets in New York at midday on September 16, killing 38 people and injuring another 300, many Americans did not panic, choosing instead to write off the attack as the act of a solitary fanatic rather than the opening volley in an approaching communist revolution. Nevertheless, the Red Scare did have a lasting impact. It led Americans who had never given much thought to the threat of the radical left in their country to take that threat seriously. At the same time it also led to a dramatic uptick in anti-immigrant sentiment. Congress soon placed restrictions on the number of immigrants allowed to enter the United States.

A NEW NATIVISM

As the new decade dawned, Americans shifted their concerns from the war to the challenge they saw in the nation's radical element, including socialists, union organizers, and anarchist organizations. Since immigrants often seemed involved in such groups, a new wave of nativism spread. Nativists believed in favoring the interests of native-born Americans and generally feared and disliked immigrants, seeing them as a threat.

The connection between European immigrants and radicalism seemed clear to many Americans when, in 1920, a pair of first-generation Italian immigrants were arrested for robbing, then murdering a paymaster at a shoe factory in South Braintree, Massachusetts. (Braintree had been the home of Founding Father and early president, John Adams.) Their names were Nicola Sacco and Bartolomeo Vanzetti, and their case soon became a national spectacle. Whether they were actually guilty or not remains in serious doubt, but the national mood was prepared to believe in their guilt. Even the judge at their month-long trial in the summer of 1921 referred to the two Italian suspects as "anarchist bastards." The trial became more concerned with striking a blow against radicalism in America than with the facts in the particular case. While the two defendants admitted that they were both anarchists, the evidence against them was scant and typically circumstantial. Both men were found guilty and sentenced to die in the electric chair. Their executions finally took place on August 23, 1927.

Anti-Immigrant, Pro-American

Italian Americans were not the only targets of nativism in America during the 1920s. During previous decades millions of European immigrants had entered the United States with few significant obstacles. But in 1921 Congress sought to end much of that human tidal wave by passing the Emergency Immigration Act.

The new act limited the number of immigrants from any European country who would be allowed to enter the United

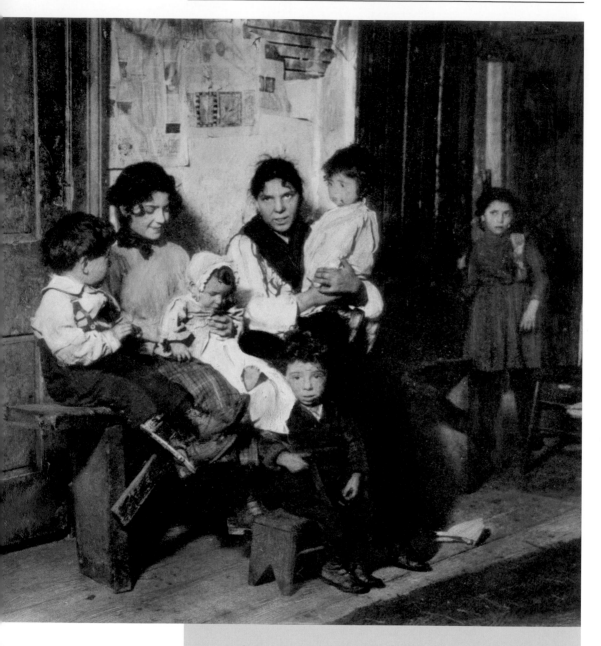

An Italian immigrant family is photographed in their Chicago home in 1910. At that time, many immigrant adults were unable to find work, and immigrant children rarely attended school.

States each year. This number was equal to just three percent of the foreign-born people of that nationality already resident in the United States, according to the information in the 1910 census. Three years later, the law was changed to two percent and based on the 1890 census numbers, since the numbers of southern and eastern Europeans in the United States were much lower then, compared to 1910. While tens of millions of immigrants had reached U.S. shores during the previous 40 years, under these new laws, only 150,000 people would be allowed to enter annually.

The message of the Emergency Immigration Act was obvious: Fewer would be allowed in and the vast majority of them, close to 85 percent, would be coming from northern and western Europe. As for Asians, the new laws closed them out completely. However, there were no restrictions on those coming from the other "Americas." Thus, the United States saw a significant rise in the number of Hispanics—primarily Cubans, Mexicans, and Puerto Ricans—into the "land of the free, home of the brave."

A Revived Ku Klux Klan

The anti-immigrant backlash in America during the 1920s found one of its loudest voices in an old organization that dated back to the years following the Civil War. The Ku Klux Klan, established in the South during the late 1860s, had intimidated blacks in an attempt to keep them from voting and claiming their equal rights. It carried out raids, assaults, and killings among black communities. The new Klan of the 1920s was still a racist organization, but one that spread its net of hate over a wider field. The Klan limited its membership to native-born, white Protestants, seeking the goal of "100 Percent Americanism." Like its predecessor, the new Klan targeted blacks, as well as Roman Catholics, Jews, immigrants, and foreigners of any kind.

Reestablished by a former Methodist minister named William J. Simmons, the Ku Klux Klan found support not only from Southerners, but from people around the country, from

ALL THAT JAZZ—AND BLUES

Among the changes witnessed during the 1920s, one of the greatest was in the field of American music. By 1920 two dominant forms of music were coming into greater popularity—jazz and the blues—and both were readily associated with African-American music styles.

Jazz had its roots in an earlier form of black music, Ragtime, which had first emerged during the 1890s. Typically it had fast-moving piano rhythms, which were borrowed from even earlier banjo syncopations. Such music was meant to be played, not sung, thus many Ragtime pieces had no words. By the early twentieth century, jazz was starting to take over Ragtime's popularity. (The earliest spelling of "jazz" was actually "jass.") Jazz was more of a blend of African and European influences, with major borrowings from nineteenth-century minstrel show tunes. Much of the music came out of New Orleans, and one of the first important jazz

musicians, Ferdinand Pechet (who would one day be known as Jelly Roll Morton) came from one of the city's French-speaking families. In 1917, he made a recording with his band, "Morton's Red Hot Peppers."

By the 1920s jazz had become a common musical style, one performed by both black and white bands. Jazz had moved northward from New Orleans, following the Mississippi River, to Memphis and St. Louis, then spread out to Kansas City and further north to Chicago. In New York jazz was performed in Harlem, which boasted the city's largest black population. Blacks and whites alike flocked to Harlem jazz clubs (where illegal liquor flowed) to hear the most popular jazz and blues performers.

One of the most fashionable music hotspots was Harlem's Cotton Club, which opened in 1923 and served a largely elite white clientele. The Cotton Club featured black singers, musicians, and waiters, who sang and

Washington state to New England. Its members still wore the white robes and white, pointed hoods, even if many members wore only a pointed cap, caring little whether their

served entirely white audiences. Such notable musicians as Cab Calloway and Edward K. "Duke" Ellington performed in this exclusive nightspot.

As for the blues, this musical form emerged from the songs written and performed by rural black Southerners who sang about their difficult lives, both economic and personal. The father of the blues, W. C. Handy, once wrote, notes historian Darlene Hine: "Southern Negroes sang about everything. Trains, steamboats, steam whistles, sledge hammers, fast women, mean bosses, stubborn mules." Blues performers typically played guitar, as well as the harmonica, and performed in rural venues from nightclubs to picnics to local fish frys. Handy wrote such important blues standards as "Memphis Blues," "Beale Street Blues," and "Careless Love."

Handy was not alone as one of the progenitors of blues music. His female counterpart was Gertrude Pridget, who sang for minstrel shows at the turn of the century, and later,

after marrying William "Pa" Rainey, became "Ma" Rainey. Prior to World War I Ma Rainey wrote and performed early blues songs, which she often based on folk ballads, spiritual hymns, and the common experiences of black folks. By the 1920s she had become known as the "Mother of the Blues."

One of the most popular African-American blues performers during the 1920s was the daughter of a Baptist preacher from Tennessee—Bessie Smith. She performed with "Ma" Rainey prior to World War I, and by the 1920s was making the rounds in clubs in Philadelphia and Atlantic City, New Jersey. In 1923, she signed a contract with Columbia Records and recorded such songs as "Down-Hearted Blues," "Gulf Coast Blues," and "Tain't Nobody's Business If I Do." In 1925 she recorded "St. Louis Blues" (W.C. Handy had written the song in 1914 and published it himself) and a song with another popular jazz performer—cornet man Louis Armstrong.

identities were kept secret or not. Simmons was rabid in his hatred of the group's targeted minorities, as well as Catholics. His public speeches portrayed these minorities as a horrific threat to white Protestant America, stating that his country was not a "melting pot" of different races, but, notes historian George Tindall, "It is a garbage can!... When the hordes of aliens walk to the ballot box and their votes outnumber yours, then that alien horde has got you by the throat."

Just how many Americans joined the Klan during the 1920s is uncertain. Estimates range from 3 to 8 million, but even those numbers might be greater than the actual number. Just as with the original Klan, its members tried to intimidate those they did not like, in an effort to try to keep their country "racially pure" and "morally straight." Nevertheless, following the passage of the 1924 immigration restriction law, the Klan began to drop in membership, since the government was taking care of the immigrant "problem" for them. Even so, in August the following year the Klan staged a massive rally in the streets of Washington, D.C., where 40,000 white-robed members—men and women—marched down Pennsylvania Avenue. Some 200,000 spectators watched the parade.

A MORAL SHIFT

While the Ku Klux Klan was generally an anti-immigrant, anti-minority, anti-Catholic organization, part of its message was that America was slipping morally. Since many Klan members were also members of Protestant denominations that were usually conservative in their moral ideals, the era's new permissivism was of great concern to them and to many other religiously conservative Americans. Some young people, including those in the middle class, were abandoning traditional moral values, and shocking their elders with their "outrageous" behaviors.

The new morality seemed most obvious among some of the nation's young women. Just after World War I the average women's skirt hung about 6 inches (15 centimeters) from the ground. In less than a decade the most liberated women were wearing skirts that showed off their knees, and then some. These women, most of them young girls in their twenties, were called "flappers." (The name was given to them by their detractors for the girls' practice of wearing their galoshes loose, allowing them to "flap" around their ankles.) Their dresses were short, filmy, and clung to the body. They cut their hair into a short bob, even as the traditional fashion had been for women to keep their hair long and rarely cut it. They smoked in public, a long-term social no-no, wore rolled silk stockings and bright red lipstick, and danced the latest dances, all with an unashamed abandon. The flappers represented a loose morality, as they and their male counterparts were known for their public displays of affection and for frequenting speakeasies, places where alcohol was served illegally. (Prohibition was in place between 1919 and 1933.)

College campuses were thought by some to represent notorious dens of immorality, where wild parties with unrestricted drinking took place and couples engaged in prolonged kissing, called "petting." Novelist F. Scott Fitzgerald wrote about such things in his fictional work, *This Side of Paradise,* published in 1920, in which a character notes how Victorian-era mothers had no "idea how casually their daughters were accustomed to be kissed."

For some Americans, the 1920s represented promiscuity and the casting off of a morality that some thought prudish and out-of-date. Just how predominant this franker, racier element of young people was in America during the 1920s remains a question. Probably it was not as extensive as some of the literature of the day seemed to indicate. The "Roaring

THE ROARING TWENTIES

The 1920s are often regarded as the beginning of modern times. In this decade, radios, cars, movie theaters, washing machines, vacuum cleaners, refrigerators, and telephones became popular. Women found more freedom to go out to work or attend university. Most people had jobs and money to spend, and they spent it by having a good time. Because of this release from the miseries of the war, the period became known as the "Roaring Twenties."

Wealthy socialites often went to nightclubs to eat, listen to live music, and dance.

Twenties" was probably only roaring for a small fraction of free-thinking individuals. By the 1930s much of that new morality had calmed down, as a generation of restless, post-war young people grew up.

A CONTINUING THIRST

Alcohol was an old American habit; Americans had always enjoyed their beer and other spirits. But, beginning around 1900, a significant campaign was underway to limit the nation's thirst for alcohol and even to ban the stuff altogether. Two organizations had led the way in opposition to booze—the Women's Christian Temperance Union and the Anti-Saloon League. In part, these organizations mirrored the morality of the Progressive Movement, which sought reforms on many levels of U.S. life. Both groups often worked hand-in-glove with Protestant denominations in the fight against alcohol and its potential evils.

The election of 1916 delivered majorities in both houses of Congress in support of an amendment to the U.S. Constitution establishing nationwide Prohibition. The war provided a further argument in its favor, with supporters calling for grain to be used as food for starving Europeans, rather than for distilling alcoholic beverages. (There were also fingers pointed at German-American brewers for their "nonpatriotic" activities.) In December 1917 Congress passed the Eighteenth Amendment, supporting Prohibition and banning the manufacture, sale, and transportation of intoxicating alcohol products. The act was ratified by the states in January 1919.

Nevertheless, the 1920s saw little decline in the level of American consumption of alcohol. Some experts even believe that drinking actually went up, given the increase in the amount of public drinking done by the era's liberated young women. In rural areas violators of the Eighteenth Amendment made moonshine [home-distilled alcohol} in remote stills, while their city cousins found it in secret taverns and lounges called speakeasies. People carried hip flasks and hid them in their clothes. Those who wanted to drink in America continued to do so, law or no law.

Prohibition and Organized Crime

Prohibition created a new, illegal market for alcohol in America, which gave rise to the era of the 1920s gangster element. Criminals, operating through organized crime groups, served as the middlemen, importing alcohol illegally from Canada, Mexico and other countries, then selling it to speakeasies. It was not that organized crime had not already existed in the United States prior to Prohibition. Such criminal activities as prostitution rings, illegal gambling, and extortion rackets had been practiced by criminal groups since the nineteenth century. But Prohibition brought a new element to the equation, and high profits could be made by those who dominated a lucrative urban market.

This led to rival criminal organizations who fought for control of "turf" in big cities, and to an era of colorful, if dangerous, criminals. The most famous was Chicago's Al "Scarface" Capone, the son of Italian immigrants, who worked his way up from nightclub bouncer to become kingpin of the largest organized crime element of his day. In 1927 alone Capone's criminal activities netted him a personal profit of $60 million through gambling, prostitution, and, most of all, smuggling illegal booze.

When others tried to "muscle" in on Capone's criminal territory, out came the submachine guns. Chicago police were left to clean up after rival gangs shot one another in alleys, on the streets, and in public joints and garages. As for Capone, he was driven around the city in a bulletproof Cadillac, with a number of well-armed bodyguards. Capone bribed officials to allow him to stay in business, or killed those who stood in his way. In the late 1920s his empire came crashing down when he was finally arrested, tried, and sentenced to 11 years in prison, not for any of his unsavory criminal activities, but for tax evasion. After all, Capone never paid taxes on monies he made illegally.

By the early 1930s Prohibition was being criticized as a failure—a well-intended experiment in support of a "dry" America. In 1931 a federal commission was formed to study the impact of Prohibition. The study observed that the law had never been fully enforced and was probably not enforceable. Alcohol consumption had remained high, and organized crime appeared to profit from it all. Yet the commission decided to stick with Prohibition, and the law remained in effect for another two years. Even as the law intended to keep America sober, the Twenties proved, for some, to be "roaring," indeed.

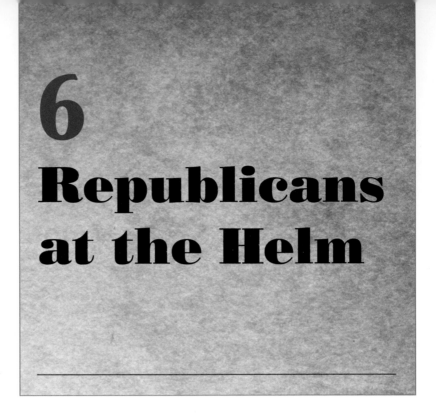

6
Republicans at the Helm

With the end of the First World War and the failure of Wilson's campaign to rally the American people behind his League of Nations and the Versailles Treaty, the Republicans thought they had great possibilities of gaining the reins of power in the 1920 election. The mood of the country had shifted dramatically since Wilson had first been elected in 1912. The demands of the Progressives did not interest as many Americans as they once had. Many people believed great strides had already been made—after all, at least five Progressive amendments had been added to the Constitution, and countless laws had been passed to regulate abuses and advocate government protections. Reform seemed a thing of the past.

The war was over, and many in the country seemed ready to put the experience in America's past. Many demands had been placed upon the American people during Wilson's crusade to save European civilization. Lives had been lost. The country was ready for a change, for a respite from obligations, both domestic and foreign. A new decade signaled an opportunity to take a step back toward a simpler time and a more relaxed mood.

A RETURN TO NORMALCY

The Republicans believed they understood the pulse of the nation in 1920. They met at their convention in Chicago to nominate a candidate. Less on the convention floor and more in "smoke-filled" backrooms, the party chose its standard bearer for the new decade, a grandfatherly figure with a manly patrician appearance from small-town America— Warren Gamaliel Harding.

The 54-year-old Harding (he would turn 55 at the time of the election) was a former newspaper publisher from Marion, Ohio, who was serving his state as a U.S senator. His role in the Senate had never been important; he was more of a low-key backbencher than a forceful voice of the people. He had never proposed an important law or policy, or even managed to give a memorable speech. He was so simplistic by nature that he was easily confused by the bigger issues—tax policies, tariff issues, and, most certainly, foreign policy. That was just what the Old Guard Republicans wanted: Someone they could rely on to do little and say less.

Harding had no grand agenda or plan for the country, which he made clear in a speech in Boston, as historian George Tindall notes:

> *America's present need is not heroics, but healing; not nostrums but normalcy; not revolution, but restoration; not agitation, but adjustment; not surgery, but serenity; not the dramatic, but the dispassionate; not experiment, but equipoise, not submergence in internationality, but sustainment in triumphant nationality.*

The postwar years saw the country return to normality and an interest in sport being rekindled. Arguably the greatest baseball player of all time, Babe Ruth, had his best season in 1921.

These were not the sort of words to be found in a speech delivered by Woodrow Wilson; just the opposite. In fact, "normalcy" was not even a word at that time. Harding meant "normality," but his misused word is now in the dictionary. Nevertheless that is what many people in America wanted: A quieter time, following loud campaigns for change, and deadly crusading through war.

To round out the ticket, the Republicans nominated Calvin Coolidge, who hailed from another small town, this time in Vermont. Just as conservative as Harding, Coolidge had been elected governor of Massachusetts in 1919 and had made national headlines that year, speaking out against a police strike in Boston. His words won the admiration of many across the country: "There is no right to strike against the public safety by anybody, anywhere, anytime."

During the campaign, Harding claimed he was a common man, the son of an Ohio farmer. In his words, "just a plain fellow… old-fashioned and even reactionary in matters of faith and morals." But in his private life, and in secrecy, Harding was a different person. Despite Prohibition, he drank bootleg whiskey. He smoked and chewed tobacco, played poker with his buddies every week, and even kept a mistress. But to so many Americans, he was charming, arrow-straight, handsome in an elderly statesman style, and everyone's favorite grandfather. He knew people liked him. He said on one occasion: "I cannot hope to be one of the great presidents, but perhaps I may be remembered as one of the best loved."

Cox and Roosevelt

With no incumbent to nominate, the Democrats landed on James M. Cox. Like Harding, he was a former Ohio newspaperman, but a governor, rather than a senator. He was a compromise candidate, as he failed to receive his party's nomination until delegates cast their 44th ballot. With the progressive Cox a bit short of an engaging personality, party leaders tried to jazz up the ticket by nominating a young New Yorker whose last name everyone in America knew— Franklin Roosevelt. Franklin Roosevelt was related to Theodore Roosevelt, and the former president had even married Franklin and his young bride, Eleanor, a distant cousin. As had TR a generation earlier, Franklin had served as assistant secretary of the Navy, under Woodrow Wilson.

But it was not yet Franklin Roosevelt's time for national office. The voters chose change, which they believed the Republicans represented. Sixty percent of the electorate cast their ballots for Harding-Coolidge. The Republicans also gained large majorities in both the House and Senate, which represented one of the most solid and complete party victories in the history of U.S. national politics. The likeable Harding had managed to charm enough voters to carry every state outside the Democratic "Solid South," and he even managed to take Tennessee. His numbers were stunning: 404 electoral votes to Cox's 127, and 16.1 million votes to the Democratic candidate's 9.1 million. The perennial Socialist candidate, Eugene V. Debs, once again polled almost 1 million votes, just as he had done in 1912.

TOO LITTLE TALENT, TOO MUCH JOB

Harding took office with his slogan intact—"A Return to Normalcy." And he intended to live up to it. He had no intention of rocking the boat, or leading the country where it might not want to go. He favored letting everything take its natural course, keeping the role of government to a minimum by not interfering with the directions of the business world or by sticking his fingers into the complicated affairs of other nations. Normalcy, as Harding meant it, was to lead his countrymen back to a simpler time with its uncomplicated politics.

In some respects, this approach by the new president did not demand much of him at all. It was just as well. Harding knew so little that he even wrote early in his term to a friend, notes historian Carter Smith: "I don't know what to do or where to go. Somewhere there must be a book that talks all about it." His relaxed conservatism didn't require a well laid out set of policies. He would simply do less by instigating fewer. Through his presidency, Harding was content to basically turn the leadership of the country over to the Republicans in Congress, who soon set a conservative course that included eliminating wartime controls on business, tax cuts, higher tariffs, and tighter immigration policies.

To help administer his "hands off" politics, Harding chose men for his cabinet who were friendly toward the practices of the nation's industrial and business movers and shakers. His most significant appointment was Andrew Mellon from Pennsylvania, a top banker and owner of the only significant company producing aluminum in America at that time. Mellon did manage to put together several pieces of the small amount of legislation that the Harding administration brought before Congress. His most important bill was one that cut income tax rates for the wealthy from a high of 65 percent down to 25 percent. He also cooperated with Congress on higher tariffs.

But such legislation was less important during the Harding years than his conservative approach and his relaxed federal handle on the nation's business sector. Harding did almost nothing to regulate big business. He did not remove the existing, established regulatory agencies, such as the Interstate Commerce Commission or the Federal Reserve Board. But he appointed men to run these and other agencies who would not upset the apple cart. They cooperated with large corporations and rarely administered existing laws against them. When they did, they used a gentle hand.

The "Ohio Gang"

Harding's limits as president also extended to those with whom he surrounded himself. He brought to Washington a group of friends and cronies whom the press soon called "the Ohio Gang." They included Harry Daugherty, who had run Republican Ohio politics as a party boss and had pushed Harding as a presidential candidate. Daugherty served as the new President's attorney general. Harding picked another buddy, New Mexico Senator Albert B. Fall, as his secretary of the Interior. Fall and Daugherty would soon prove poor choices for such important government posts, as they both became involved in fraud and corruption.

Several scandals began to rock the Harding Administration in 1923. Harding learned that year that his head of the Veterans Bureau was stealing and reselling medical supplies and hospital equipment. When the scandal was exposed, the official hightailed it to Europe to avoid prosecution. Caught in another scandal, Harding's general counsel shot himself. Another suicide took place when one of Attorney General Daugherty's close associates also killed himself with a handgun. Though not an official of Harding's, he had been selling his influence in the administration for money. Daugherty himself was implicated in a scandal involving German assets that the Allies had seized after World War I. Due to a lack of evidence and his refusal to testify due to self-incrimination (a tactic involving invoking the Fifth Amendment), Daugherty was never indicted, much less convicted of any crime, even though prosecutors tried on two occasions.

Illegal Loans

The most significant scandal proved to be the one involving Albert Fall. It was discovered, partially through a Senate investigation, that Fall had arranged through his Interior Department to open up a pair of western oil reserves for private use. The two federal reserves, Elk Hills in California and Teapot Dome in Wyoming, had earlier been set aside as naval oil reserves. Fall had transferred control of those reserves from the navy to the Interior Department, then leased them secretly to private oil interests, including Sinclair Oil of California. In return, the Interior Secretary received nearly $500,000 in "loans," a claim he continued to make for the rest of his life. But Fall was indicted, convicted, and went to prison for a year. He was the first Cabinet member in U.S. history to be put behind bars while still holding his office.

Federal Prohibition agents carry out a bootleg liquor raid at a restaurant in 1923. America had become "dry" on January 16, 1920. However, there was much illegal importing of liquor from Canada and Mexico.

As these scandals and others began to break in the summer of 1923, Harding was bemused and concerned. Although he was never personally involved in any of these dark deeds and events, they troubled him greatly, leading him to tell a journalist: "I have no trouble with my enemies, I can take care of my enemies all right. But my damn friends… they're the ones that keep me walking the floor nights!"

Harding's Legacy

Harding did not have to worry long about the failures and illegalities of his appointees. In the summer of 1923 he went on a speaking tour out West, visiting several states and the Alaska Territory. During his sail north he asked his Secretary of Commerce, Herbert Hoover, that, if he were president, would he make public to the press a scandal in his administration if he knew of one or would he hide it, hoping the public never found out? Hoover was straightforward: "Publish

A MAN OF GOOD REPUTE

Born of Quaker parents in 1874, Herbert Hoover had first become a national figure during World War I. A successful mining engineer (he and his wife, Lou Henry, had both graduated from Stanford University with geology degrees), he had worked around the world, including in China, and accumulated a personal fortune of $4 million by 1914. When the war broke out he was tapped to lead the government's

Food Administration—a humanitarian food program for those displaced by the European conflict. Appointed by Woodrow Wilson, Hoover worked in this role throughout the war, refusing any compensation for his efforts. So successful were the Hoover food aid programs that his future presidential rival Franklin Roosevelt was prompted to sing his praises: "He certainly is a wonder, and I wish we could make him president of the United States."

it, and at least get credit for integrity on your side." But the question was soon moot, for Harding died in San Francisco on his way back from Alaska, struck down by a heart attack. His body was later sent back east by train and millions of mourning Americans lined the tracks. Not since Lincoln's death had the U.S. public responded with such emotion to the passing of a president.

Soon, however, the scandals began to break, and Harding became less the object of sadness and more the target of ridicule and scorn. And the scandals continued to unfold for almost a decade after his death. Even his extramarital affairs became public knowledge. Many historians today look on the Harding administration as one of the worst and certainly most corrupt in U.S. history. In rankings by historians, the often befuddled Harding typically comes in last among his fellow presidents. Even then, he is not always considered a complete failure as the nation's chief executive. Some credit him with leading the country through the transition from wartime to peacetime and helping the economy to grow through his conservative economic policies, which may have fueled a postwar boom. He was hard working and well meaning, yet not universally sound in his judgments, especially in the people he chose for his cabinet and other advisors. While Harding had relatively stumbled his way through his presidency until his death, he had managed to make four Supreme Court appointments during his two-and-a-half years in the White House. Largely conservative picks, these appointments included former president William Howard Taft.

COOLIDGE TAKES THE LEADERSHIP

With Harding's death, Vice President Calvin Coolidge took the executive leadership of the country. He first received word of the president's passing while visiting his father in the mountains of Plymouth, Vermont, where he was born. Colonel John Coolidge, a 78-year-old justice of the peace, swore in his son as president in his house at 2:47 A.M. by the light of a kerosene lamp. Although the new chief executive later took the oath of office during a formal ceremony in Washington, the simple circumstances of his first swearing in at his father's side evoked the simple nature of Calvin Coolidge.

He was not Harding in many ways. Harding might not have been personally dishonest, but he had tolerated those who had been. Coolidge was the epitome of honesty. He was also as low-key an individual as has likely ever served as a U.S. president. He was a quiet and reserved individual, one who kept his own counsel, with a personality that bordered on the bland. Although quite talkative with his close friends, he had a reputation as a man of few public words, gaining him the nickname "Silent Cal." If Harding had been careless with women and alcohol, Coolidge was puritanical.

But Harding and Coolidge were similar in their approach to governing. Coolidge felt the smaller the government, the better. He was a non-interventionist concerning the economy and spent his years as president doing as little as possible. He insisted, almost without exception, in getting 12 hours of sleep a night, then taking a nap each afternoon. His critics accused him of practically sleeping through his presidency. Throughout the remainder of Harding's term, Coolidge continued his predecessor's course of minimal government and *laissez faire* economics. He was quoted saying: "The chief business of America is business." He did not even change most of Harding's appointees.

The 1924 Election
Come 1924 Coolidge had the opportunity to be elected president in his own right. The Republicans were more than

willing to stick with Silent Cal. The Democrats were, unfortunately for them, woefully split that year. With Prohibition still in place, the Democrats included a faction that wanted to maintain the course of banning alcohol. This group included the rural South and conservative westerners. These "Drys" supported the perennial candidate, William Jennings Bryan, who had first run for president back in 1896. The "Wets" wanted to do away with Prohibition and took their support from urban centers and immigrants. At the convention, delegates cast 103 ballots before they finally locked in on a compromise candidate, a Wall Street lawyer from West Virginia, John W. Davis.

Both Coolidge and Davis were conservative candidates, which upset those who still longed for the days when Progressives could carry an election. A third party was established, nominating longtime reform leader, Robert LaFollette from Wisconsin, who was by then 70 years old. Coolidge chose to campaign hardest against LaFollette, telling the U.S. electorate that the Progressive diehard was "dangerous" and wanted to convert the United States into "a communistic and socialistic state." On election day Coolidge kept his office, garnering 15 million votes to Davis's 8.5 million and LaFollette's 5 million, as Americans followed the Republicans' slogan: "Keep Cool With Coolidge." The Democrat candidate had only managed to accumulate one out of every three votes.

COOLIDGE CONTINUES

Coolidge's second term was largely a mirror image of his first, but without the holdover scandals of the Harding years. The administration continued to support high tariffs, low corporate taxes, and a do-nothing policy concerning trusts. Although farmers were beginning to see economic problems during the late 1920s, ahead of the curve of the approaching Great Depression, Coolidge did little but veto bills intended to provide farm support. He also vetoed a bill that would have established bonuses for World War I veterans. Through all these conservative moves, Coolidge remained extremely popular with the American people.

Despite Coolidge's conservative approach, there were some necessary responses to the progress the country was experiencing at the time. Congress passed the Air Commerce Act, which required the registration of all airplane pilots. Also, the government created the Federal Radio Commission to regulate the rapidly expanding radio industry. (In 1934, the FRC became the Federal Communications Commission.)

Radios became popular during the 1920s, with the first station, KDKA in Pittsburgh, coming on the airwaves in 1920. In 1922 there were only four stations broadcasting, but the following year ended with 566 in operation. Hundreds of thousands of U.S. households were listening in. Then, in 1926, the Radio Corporation of America (RCA) established the first national network of stations, the National Broadcasting Company (NBC), with broadcast signals carried by telephone wires. NBC carried two networks, the "red" and the "blue," including such sponsored programs as The Maxwell House Hour and the Ipana Troubadours, paid for by a popular toothpaste company.

A POPULAR NEW PRESIDENT

Coolidge kept his popularity during his second term and could have run for a third, but decided not to do so. The Republicans turned to yet another conservative leader of their party, Commerce Secretary Herbert Hoover. The Democrats came to the 1928 election with fewer splits than they had faced in 1924. They nominated New York Governor Alfred E. Smith, a gregarious, cigar-chomping Irish-Catholic.

The two men were stark contrasts. Hoover was as taciturn, even gloomy appearing as Coolidge. He wore tailored blue suits and appeared the grand symbol of stability and conservative values. Smith was an outgoing, talkative politician who spoke with a New York urban twang. He wore loud, checkered suits and a brown derby. Unfortunately, he had not made it clear to party officials that he supported the end of Prohibition until he had already been nominated. This fact caused him to lose support from rural voters, especially among Southerners. The two men did not differ much, however, on economic policies. Their differences were largely a matter of political style.

In the election Hoover won by a landslide, taking 58 percent of the vote. He managed to cut into traditional Democratic territory by winning six Southern states. In all, Hoover won 21 million votes, 6 million more than Coolidge had four years earlier. Few presidents in U.S. history would enter the White House on the wave of such popularity.

7

A New American Culture

For many Americans, the 1920s would prove confusing and difficult, despite their relative prosperity. While the Allies had united on the battlefield against the Central Powers, they had only managed to squabble at Versailles, often over issues that Americans did not fully understand or even care about directly. The country had itself united on behalf of the war effort, but, once the great conflict was over, old issues and social clashes emerged once again, joined by several new ones to boot. As historian James Kirby Martin notes: "Wets battled drys, atheists ridiculed fundamentalists, white, Anglo-Saxon Protestants (WASPs) denounced the 'new immigrants,' whites lashed out against blacks, and practically everyone sensed a decline in morality." Those living on the farms thought city folks lacked moral fiber. Farmers still fought big business and industrial development. Those on the East Coast could not imagine the lives of the provincials living in the South and the Midwest.

Yet much of the criticism between U.S. social, economic, and regional groups had less to do with disliking the other guy and more to do with moving into an era of uncertainty. What would the future America look like? Would it cling to its traditional values and beliefs? Or was the country being thrust into a whole new transitional era, which might even increase the gaps that already existed between its various groups and factions?

NEW LEVELS OF URBANIZATION

During the 1920s America found itself in the midst of greater urbanization. Cities were on the rise, as the 1920 census indicated, and the balance between city and country was tipping. That year more Americans lived in cities than in rural areas. Granted, many more of the urban class were living in small towns than in great metropolitan areas, but more and more people were also living in cities greater than 50,000 in population. Throughout the decade approximately 15 million Americans moved from rural to urban areas. The majority of these new urbanites were not newly arrived immigrants, but people who were trading country living for city dwelling. Even though the South remained predominantly rural, the region still saw the largest level of urbanization in the nation. In 1920 one out of every four Southerners lived in an urban area. By 1930 the numbers had shifted to one in three.

BLACK MOBILITY

Among those Southerners who moved to urban areas during the 1920s were large numbers of blacks. In 1910 75 percent of American blacks had lived in rural areas and 90 percent of them lived in the South. But during and after World War I those demographics began to change. Making efforts to escape the traditional harsh realities of Southern rural life, with its sharecropping, 1.5 million blacks moved to urban centers during the 1920s. Some remained in the South, taking residence in Birmingham, Memphis, Atlanta, and other cities. But the lion's share moved to northern urban centers— New York, Philadelphia, St. Louis, Cleveland, Chicago, and Cincinnati. By the end of the 1920s, 20 percent of American blacks lived in the North.

But not all was rosy for blacks who left the South in search of better circumstances and greater opportunities. They moved in such numbers that housing shortages were a problem, especially in areas where whites did not allow them to take residence in traditionally "white" neighborhoods. The segregation that had become a metaphor for mistreatment in the South was also practiced in the North.

The U.S. Supreme Court declared "municipal residential segregation ordinances" unconstitutional in 1917, but whites soon began forming "restrictive covenants" to continue closing off white neighborhoods to blacks. Under such agreements white property owners could not legally sell their land, businesses, or houses to blacks. If they did, they could be sued by their neighbors. The Supreme Court finally caught up with that practice in 1948, declaring such covenants illegal. Despite such restrictive efforts by whites, black communities sprang up and thrived across the North. By 1930 whole neighborhoods in such cities as Chicago, Philadelphia, and New York were more than 90 percent black.

RACIAL DEFIANCE

Even though the racism that blacks experienced during the 1920s was nothing new, the decade did witness a change in the responses of black Americans to continuing, unrelenting discrimination. While earlier black leaders, such as Booker T. Washington, had encouraged those of his race to remain friendly to whites, even complicit at times, some elements of the black community were now prepared to challenge white authority. In 1911 black social workers and others, including conservative blacks, formed the National Urban League (NUL), its purpose being to help blacks find employment. Despite its intentions, such organizations as the NUL did not make a serious dent in the employment status of the nation's black workers.

Perhaps the most significant black organization during the 1920s was one founded a decade earlier. The National Association for the Advancement of Colored People (NAACP) had been organized in 1909 and its intentions were to challenge existing laws that limited the civil rights of America's black people. It was the NAACP whose lawyers won the Supreme Court decision against restrictive covenants in 1917 and the elimination in 1915 of "grandfather clauses" that had limited voting privileges.

Ironically, the original organization had been headed by white liberals, but after the Great War blacks took over the top positions of leadership within the NAACP. The organization's first black secretary (leader), James Weldon Johnson, led the organization's members during the 1920s in campaigns against segregation in Northern urban schools. He also struggled less successfully on behalf of a federal anti-lynching law. It was during the 1920s and early 1930s that the NAACP became the country's leading civil rights organization.

Yet some blacks in America were more radicalized than the NUL or the NAACP and set out on their own agenda. One of these maverick leaders was A. Philip Randolph, who organized one of the first black trade unions in America— the Brotherhood of Sleeping Car Porters—during the 1920s. His fight was long and hard. The Pullman Company did not even recognize the Brotherhood as the bargaining agent for its porters until 1937.

A hand-colored photograph of Marcus Garvey (1887–1940). In 1920 Garvey organized a month-long meeting in New York City for black leaders from across the United States. On the agenda was a bill of rights for blacks.

"Africa for the Africans"

While Randolph tried to speak on behalf of the larger population of blacks in America, he was typically best accepted by the more elite group of blacks, those with higher educations. Perhaps a more unique voice for the mass black audience in America was a charismatic Jamaican immigrant named Marcus Garvey, who preached a different sort of message. Though other black leaders in America were calling for racial integration, Garvey rejected the idea, extolling instead the uniqueness of the black race and the need to keep it separate from others.

Garvey, who often dressed publicly in a military uniform complete with plumed hat, claimed that God and Jesus were both black, that Africa was the cradle of civilization and that, in so many words, "black is beautiful." Garvey encouraged blacks to buy only from black-operated businesses. He and others opened several such storefronts, including a doll factory that only made black dolls. He formed the Universal Negro Improvement Association in 1914 and pushed for American blacks to emigrate "back" to Africa, his slogan stating: "Africa for the Africans, at home and abroad." To facilitate the colonization of blacks to Africa, Garvey sold stock in a black steamship company, but was in time accused of fraud and misuse of funds, and served a short stint in jail. In 1927 the U.S. government deported him back to Jamaica, where he died forgotten in 1940.

The "New Negro"

Despite his failures, Marcus Garvey had struck a nerve. He had tapped into a growing trend among American blacks to take pride in themselves and their race. After centuries of being beaten down, the time had come for the black race to stand up for itself and project its best talents to the forefront. Black pride meant, also, that blacks accepted everything about themselves that made them black. Magazines that blacks read during the 1920s were filled with advertisements for cosmetics to lighten skin and straighten hair, treatments designed to help blacks feel more accepted by white society and to distance themselves from their racial roots and identity. But black pride was now on the march.

One of the great centers for black nationalism was New York's Harlem, on upper Manhattan. There, poets and other writers, as well as artists, expressed this new spirit through their talents. Claude McKay (*Home to Harlem*, 1928), another Jamaican immigrant, led the movement, which came to be called the "Harlem Renaissance." McKay tried to portray the traditional culture of black folk, through such poems as *If We Must Die* and *To the White Fiends*. He was soon joined by such writers as Langston Hughes (*The Negro Speaks of Rivers*, 1921 and *The Weary Blues*, 1926), Wallace Thurman, Countee Cullen (*Color*, 1925 and *Copper Sun*, 1927), Zora Neale Hurston (*Their Eyes Were Watching God*, 1937) and James Weldon Johnson. During the late 1920s, Hughes, Thurman, and Hurston all lived in the same rooming house at 267 West 136 Street. The movement is thought to have originated during World War I. *The New York Herald Tribune* made note of it in a 1925 issue, notes historian Rebecca Ferguson: "We are on the edge, if not in the midst, of what might not improperly be called a Negro Renaissance."

Langston Hughes became known for his poetry, essays, and other works through which he defended the realism and authenticity of black literature. In one poem he included the line: "I am a Negro—and beautiful." A leading novel (it is more of a collection of short stories, vignettes, and poems) of the movement was *Cane* (1923), written by Jean Toomer, which presented the contrasts between poor rural blacks who worked the sawmills of Georgia during the 1880s and more well-to-do middle-class blacks in Washington, D.C.

For all the talent represented in the Harlem Renaissance, its impact was largely limited to an elite audience of blacks and whites. Langston Hughes even noted, in Harold Cruse's book, *The Crisis of the Negro Intellectual:* "The ordinary Negroes hadn't heard of the Negro Renaissance. And if they had, it hadn't raised their wages any." In addition, some critics claimed that the emphasis placed by the movement on presenting black folk stories and primitive presentations of blacks only furthered stereotypes of blacks held by whites. But the movement gave blacks a voice—and one of significant talent—where few such voices had existed previously. In the end, those literary artists of the Harlem Renaissance were having the same impact on a broader U.S. culture that the traditionally black musical forms of jazz and blues were also having during the 1920s. The message was simple: American blacks had something to say and something to contribute.

A NEW AMERICAN LITERATURE

While black writers were finding a voice of expression for their race, other writers were also busy during the 1920s, penning their interpretations of life in the United States. Some were disappointed in the directions their nation had taken during the previous generation and sought to expose modern America as a society too greedy for dollars and prone to violence and war. Others were aware of the transitional nature of their times, that the new concept of "modern" was based, in part, on recognizing that the world was in constant motion, in a constant state of change, and that the values of the past were just that—past.

American-in-exile Gertrude Stein, who spent much of her adult life in Paris, once wrote: "One must never forget that the reality of the twentieth century is not the reality of the nineteenth century, not at all." It was Stein who told such

AUTOMOBILES AND AIRPLANES

The 1920s produced many technological innovations that represented major advancements in such fields as communications, transportation, and industrialization. Two were significant standouts, each of which brought great change to life in the United States—automobiles and airplanes. Neither was invented during the 1920s, but decades earlier. Yet both found their niches during the decade, becoming popular symbols of what the modern world would include.

In the 1920s such automobile innovators as Henry Ford created assembly lines capable of churning out millions of automobiles, and producing them so inexpensively that nearly everyone in America could afford one. Ford made certain that his workers could buy the very cars they were making by paying his employees $5 a day, a good wage at that time. In the 1920s a standard Model-T Ford cost about $300. By 1930, Ford and other auto companies in the United States had created an industry that provided jobs for 4 million people, while jamming America's streets and highways with millions of simple, yet dependable, cars.

Even greater innovations could be found in the development of the nation's early airplanes. First invented in 1903 by Orville and Wilbur Wright, planes were retooled and improved, and sent to the front during World War I, changing the nature of modern-day war. It was due to the war that the airplane industry took off, with two dozen airplane plants operating, producing 20,000 planes annually. Airplanes became part of the nation's navy and army, while other planes carried the nation's mail and light cargo from coast-to-coast. Airplane flights covered distances in hours that had previously only been spanned in days or even weeks.

No greater name was associated with airplane travel during the 1920s than that of Charles Lindbergh, a young mail pilot who flew the first solo, non-stop flight from New York to Paris on May 21–22, 1927. Lindbergh's entire transatlantic flight was accomplished in only 33 hours. A similar journey by ship took about 6 days.

young writers as Sherwood Anderson and Ernest Hemingway: "All of you young people who served in the war, you are the lost generation." This "lost" generation of writers saw themselves as men and women of expression, not just mimickers of social norms and expectations. They were there to question the status quo. And question they did.

The first American writer to win the Nobel Prize for literature, Sinclair Lewis, wrote a trilogy of novels—*Main Street* (1920), *Babbitt* (1922), and *Arrowsmith* (1925)—in which he criticized America's capitalistic middle class. In *Babbitt*, Lewis noted the growing impact that modern advertising methods were having on a naïve U.S. society: "These standard advertised wares—toothpastes, socks, tires, cameras, instantaneous hot water heaters—were the symbols and proofs of excellence." Similarly, Midwest-born F. Scott Fitzgerald wrote his novel *The Great Gatsby* (1925) as an indictment of the nation's lust for material wealth and the vacuous nature of a generation of young Americans who no longer maintained an accurate moral compass.

As for Hemingway, who had driven an ambulance in the Eastern theater of the war, he wrote about a world he perceived no longer had any meaning. Jaded by his wartime experiences, uncertain whether the war had accomplished anything noble or even useful, Hemingway wrote novels as a means of healing his scars, both physical and psychological. In 1926, his book *The Sun Also Rises* portrayed his "lost" generation of Americans living in Paris, trying to squeeze meaning out of their existences by frequenting French street cafes and Spanish bull fights. His second novel, *A Farewell to Arms* (1929), was semi-autobiographical, as were many of his literary works. It focuses on a young American ambulance driver in Italy who leaves the war and flees to Switzerland with his lover, a nurse, who dies in childbirth at the book's end. The book's theme—making sense of a world that no longer makes any sense—would serve as a sounding board for later Hemingway works, as well as the writings of an entire generation.

AT THE MOVIES

The writings of the "Lost Generation" of Fitzgerald, Hemingway, Lewis, and others had a singular impact on the American reading public during the 1920s, just as their black counterparts in the Harlem Renaissance had their own impact. But many more Americans were taking in a new medium that was beginning to reach a new stride during the postwar decade—motion pictures. Thomas Alva Edison had first invented the motion picture camera in 1896, but it would not be until the years prior to the Great War that the movie industry began to take serious shape.

Then, in 1915, a monumental film by director D. W. Griffith hit the nation's big screens: *The Birth of a Nation*. It was a multi-reel extravaganza that presented Griffith's take on U.S. history, complete with a sympathetic presentation of the Ku Klux Klan. President Woodrow Wilson loved the film, as did the countless thousands of ordinary Americans who went to see it. Soon movie theaters were opening across the country in thousands of cities and small towns. By the 1930s the motion picture industry was employing half a million people and had invested more than $2 billion in film equipment, costumes, movie sets, and stars' salaries.

Through the 1910s and the 1920s motion pictures were limited entertainment forms. They were silent; the first talking motion picture, known as a "Talkie," was *The Jazz Singer*, released in 1927. Most were short, lasting only minutes or no more than an hour. There were westerns, pirate films, historical epics, adaptations of classic literature, and endless comedies—two-reel films produced by Mack Sennett's Keystone Studios, that featured silent film era comedians such as Buster Keaton, Charlie Chaplin, Harold Lloyd, and Sennett's kinetic cast called the Keystone Cops.

Each week 100 million Americans went to 20,000 theaters to watch silent pictures. Studios grew, including Paramount Pictures and Louis B. Mayer's motion picture company, Metro-Goldwyn-Mayer (MGM). These studios produced more and more elaborate films and created box-office film stars, such as heartthrob Rudolph Valentino. After his sudden death in 1926, thousands of sobbing fans attended his funeral in New York, the line of mourners stretching down the street for eight blocks.

THE COMING STORM

Without question, the United States that had entered the Great War in 1917 and the nation that emerged near the close of the 1920s were very different. The country had experienced great change in a short period of time, perhaps more than in any other era in its history. The 1920s represented a spider's web of change and adaptation, international disillusion, new hope in technology, extravagant consumption, and inward soul-searching. So much that had been in America had been lost, yet much of that loss was tempered by a U.S. economy that, to all appearances, had brought unbelievable and unrivaled prosperity. As the decade had roared forward its industrial base churned out unbelievable amounts of consumer goods, improving the lives and the standard of living of the nation's citizens, both young and old.

But even as the last days of the 1920s approached, change was again in the wind. An economic storm lay across America's horizon and much of the prosperity that had helped to define a decade would be lost in the tumult of a thundering stock market crash.

Chronology

1914

> *June* Franz Ferdinand, heir to the Austro-Hungarian throne, is assassinated in Sarajevo, which leads to World War I
>
> *August* World War I begins between the major and minor nations of Europe, as well as Asia

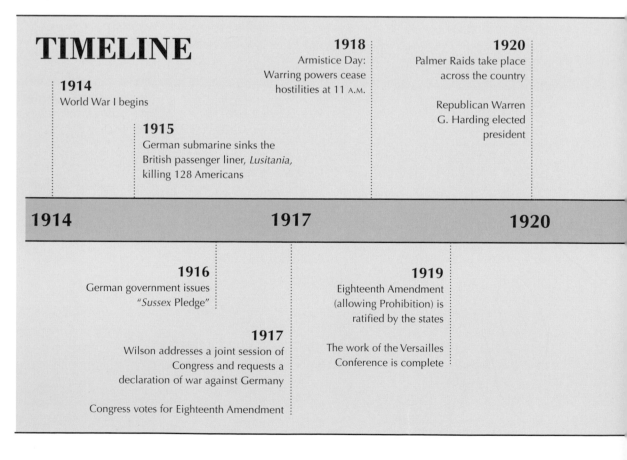

TIMELINE

1914
World War I begins

1915
German submarine sinks the British passenger liner, *Lusitania*, killing 128 Americans

1918
Armistice Day: Warring powers cease hostilities at 11 A.M.

1920
Palmer Raids take place across the country

Republican Warren G. Harding elected president

1914 **1917** **1920**

1916
German government issues "*Sussex* Pledge"

1917
Wilson addresses a joint session of Congress and requests a declaration of war against Germany

Congress votes for Eighteenth Amendment

1919
Eighteenth Amendment (allowing Prohibition) is ratified by the states

The work of the Versailles Conference is complete

1915

May German submarine sinks the British passenger liner, *Lusitania*, killing 128 Americans

August British passenger liner, *Arabic*, is sunk by a German submarine

September German government issues the "*Arabic* Pledge"

1916 Major battles of Verdun and the Somme are fought

March German submarine sinks the French passenger liner, *Sussex*, killing four Americans

May German government issues "*Sussex* Pledge"

November Wilson reelected, winning campaign against Republican Charles Evans Hughes

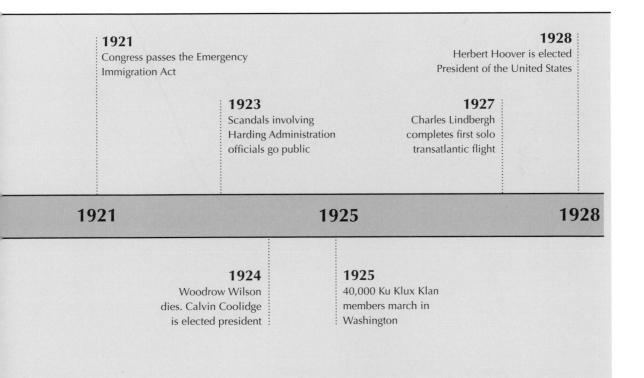

1921
Congress passes the Emergency Immigration Act

1923
Scandals involving Harding Administration officials go public

1927
Charles Lindbergh completes first solo transatlantic flight

1928
Herbert Hoover is elected President of the United States

1921   **1925**   **1928**

1924
Woodrow Wilson dies. Calvin Coolidge is elected president

1925
40,000 Ku Klux Klan members march in Washington

1917

> *January 31* Germany announces resumption of unrestricted submarine warfare
>
> *February 3* President Wilson severs diplomatic ties with Germany
>
> *March 1* Zimmerman Telegram is made public to the American people
>
> *March 17* U.S. merchant ships *Illinois* and *City of Memphis* sunk by German U-Boats
>
> *April 2* Wilson addresses a joint session of Congress and requests a declaration of war against Germany
>
> *April 6* Congress officially declares war on Germany
>
> *May* Congress adopts the Selective Service Act
>
> *June* Congress passes the Espionage Act
>
> *December* Congress votes for Eighteenth Amendment

1918 Worldwide spread of Spanish Flu infects millions

> *January* Wilson presents his 14 Points to Congress
>
> *March* Germans launch major "Peace Offensive" involving 62 German regiments
>
> *April* Wilson establishes the National War Labor Board
>
> *May* Congress passes the Sedition Act. U.S. Army's First Division captures French town of Cantigny. U.S. Third Division holds off Germans at Chateau-Thierry
>
> *June* U.S. Army's Second Division battles Germans along the Marne. Later that month, U.S. Second Division and the Fourth Marine Brigade fight Germans in Belleau Wood
>
> *July* U.S. forces fight German offensive to a standstill near the French city of Reims, leading to a counterattack involving the U.S. Army's First and Second Divisions
>
> *Sept–Oct* U.S. forces battle Germans for 47 days and succeed in pushing them back

November 7 Kaiser Wilhelm II abdicates his throne and flees to Holland in exile

November 11 Armistice Day: Warring powers cease hostilities at 11 A.M.

December 4 President Wilson travels to Europe to participate in the Versailles negotiations

1919

January Eighteenth Amendment (allowing Prohibition) is ratified by the states. Versailles Conference takes up its business

June Home of Attorney General Alexander Mitchell Palmer is bombed

July The work of the Versailles Conference is complete and the treaty has been written. Wilson returns to the United States to present the treaty to the U.S. Senate for ratification. Race riots erupt across the United States

Aug–Oct Wilson takes his campaign on behalf of U.S. membership in the League of Nations to the American people

October Wilson suffers a debilitating stroke

November U.S. Justice Department engages in raids of offices of the Union of Russian Workers in a dozen cities

1920 Italian immigrants Sacco and Venzetti are arrested. F. Scott Fitzgerald's *This Side of Paradise* is published. Sinclair Lewis publishes *Main Street*

January Palmer Raids take place across the country, with more than 6,000 people taken into custody. Eighteenth Amendment goes into effect, bringing about Prohibition

May Failing ratification of the Versailles Treaty, Congress declares World War I over by a joint resolution, but Wilson vetoes the action

November Republican Warren G. Harding elected president

1921 Congress passes the Emergency Immigration Act. Sinclair Lewis publishes *Babbitt*

March Wilson leaves office and begins his retirement from public life

July Congress votes again to declare World War I over, with Harding signing the bill

1923 Scandals involving Harding Administration officials go public. Harlem's Cotton Club opens. Harding dies in August

1924 Woodrow Wilson dies. Calvin Coolidge is elected president

1925 40,000 Ku Klux Klan members march in Washington, D.C. Sinclair Lewis publishes *Arrowsmith*. F. Scott Fitzgerald publishes *The Great Gatsby*

1926 Ernest Hemingway publishes his novel, *The Sun Also Rises*

1927 Convicted radicals Sacco and Vanzetti are executed in the electric chair. U.S. government officials deport Marcus Garvey back to Jamaica. Charles Lindbergh completes first solo transatlantic flight

1928 Herbert Hoover is elected President of the United States

1929 Hemingway's novel, *A Farewell to Arms*, is published

Glossary

abdicate To renounce a throne or other high office.

alliance An association of nations formed to further certain common interests.

Alsace-Lorraine Two provinces lying between France and Germany, which have belonged at different periods to France or Germany, according to the fortunes of war.

anarchist A person who wants to abolish all forms of government.

armistice An agreement between warring opponents to suspend hostilities, in order to discuss terms for peace and settlement.

assembly line An arrangement of workers, machines, and equipment in a factory, in which the product being assembled passes consecutively from operation to operation until completed.

Big Four The leaders of the United States of America, Britain, France, and Italy—the four most influential countries after World War I. They were Woodrow Wilson, David Lloyd George, Georges Clemenceau, and Vittorio Orlando.

Blues A style of African-American music, developed in the South during the mid-1800s, which became the foundation of most subsequent American popular music.

Bolshevik A member of the extreme wing of the Russian Social Democratic Party that seized power in Russia in 1917.

casualty A person lost in battle through death, wounds, capture, or being missing in action.

colony A country or region that is ruled by another country.

Communism A political system in which all property and wealth are held in common, to be available to everyone.

czar The absolute ruler of Russia before the revolution of 1917. The title was derived from the Latin *Caesar* given to leaders of Ancient Rome.

Expansionism The policy of expanding a nation's territory.

Fourteen (14) Points Wilson's plan for the World War I peace treaty. It included freedom of the seas and the formation of the League of Nations.

front In military terms, a line or an area where armies are fighting one another. In World War I there were Eastern and Western fronts.

isolationism A national policy of abstaining from political or economic relations with other countries.

jazz A musical style, based on improvisation within a band format. Jazz combines African traditions of repetition, call and response, and strong beat with European structure.

Kaiser The Emperor of the German people from 1871 to 1918. The title derived from the Latin *Caesar*.

laissez faire A French expression, meaning "to leave alone." In economic theory, it is the principle that economies with little government involvement are the most effective.

League of Nations An alliance of nations, devised by President Wilson, set up after World War I to promote world peace.

Lost Generation A group of alienated American authors who were disillusioned with the conformity and culture of the 1920s. They included Faulkner, Fitzgerald, Hemingway, and Gertrude Stein.

mandate A commission granted by the League of Nations to a member nation for the establishment of responsible government over a conquered territory.

mobilize In military terms, to assemble troops and resources to make ready for war.

Nationalism A sense of national consciousness that exalts one nation above all others and places primary emphasis on its culture and interests as opposed to those of other nations.

nativism Discriminatory attitudes expressed against ethnic and national minorities immigrating to the United States.

neutral Not aligned with a political or ideological grouping, or with any side in a war.

normalcy A word made up by President Harding and referring to the way life was in the United States before World War I.

Palmer Raids A series of raids organized by the Department of Justice between 1919 and 1921 against suspected radical citizens and immigrants. The raids are named for Alexander Mitchell Palmer, then Attorney General.

parliamentary Of or related to rule by a parliament or assembly as the supreme legislative body.

prohibition A ban on the production, sale, and consumption of alcoholic beverages. Prohibition was established in the United States by the Eighteenth Amendment, adopted in 1919 and repealed in 1933.

radical Someone who advocates revolutionary changes in economic, political, or social practices.

reparation Compensation payable to the victor by a nation defeated in war, especially the payments demanded of Germany after World War I.

sharecropping Labor system common to blacks following the Civil War. Workers labor on another's land, with the landowner providing everything needed to farm, including a plow, mule, and seed. The worker "pays back" his debt to the landowner out of his annual harvest.

Slavic Related to the Slav peoples of eastern Europe and Russia.

Socialism A social system based on government ownership and administration of the means of production and distribution of goods.

stalemate A deadlock. The term comes from chess, where the position leads to a draw.

talkie A motion picture that has synchronized sound. Such films were introduced in the late 1920s.

tariff A payment made to a government by an importer, to allow goods to be brought into that country.

temperance Non-consumption of alcoholic beverages.

theater In military terms, a large area of land, sea, and air where war operations may take place.

Triple Alliance A mutual military treaty made before World War I between Germany, Austria-Hungary, and Italy.

Triple Entente A mutual military treaty made before World War I between Great Britain, France, and Russia. These three nations were known as the Associated (or Allied) powers during the Great War.

U-boat A German submarine designed for undersea operations.

unrestricted submarine warfare The German practice of attacking all shipping from countries it was at war with, including passenger liners. This policy annoyed neutral countries.

Versailles Conference An international conference, held after World War I at Versailles in northern Paris, to set the peace terms for Germany and other defeated nations.

Versailles Treaty The peace treaty that formally ended World War I on June 28, 1919, and in which the victorious Allies imposed punitive reparations on Germany.

Zimmermann Note A secret telegram sent by the German foreign minister, Arthur Zimmermann, to the German embassy in Mexico City in February 1917. It instructed the ambassador to convince Mexico to go to war with the United States. The message was intercepted and caused the United States to mobilize against Germany.

Bibliography

Brands, H. W. *Woodrow Wilson. The American Presidents series*. New York: Times Books, Henry Holt and Company, 2003.

Brinkley, Alan. *The Unfinished Nation*. Boston, MA: McGraw-Hill, 2000.

Chace, James. *1912: Wilson, Roosevelt, Taft and Debs: The Election That Changed the Country*. New York: Simon & Schuster, 2005.

Chambers, John Whiteclay. *The Tyranny of Change: America in the Progressive Era, 1890–1920*. New York: St. Martin's Press, 1980.

Cruse, Harold. *The Crisis of the Negro Intellectual*. Port Orchard, WA: Apollo Editions Publishing, 1970.

Ferguson, Rebecca. *The Handy History Answer Book*. Canton, MI: Visible Ink Press, 2006.

Fitzgerald, F. Scott. *This Side of Paradise*. New York: Scribners, 1920.

Grayson, Cary T. *Woodrow Wilson: An Intimate Memoir*. New York: Holt, Rinehart, and Winston, 1960.

Hine, Darlene Clark. *The African-American Odyssey*. Upper Saddle River, NJ: Prentice Hall, 2000.

Kennedy, David M. *Over Here: The First World War and American Society*. New York: Oxford University Press, 1980.

Lawson, Don. *The United States in World War I: The Story of General John J. Pershing and the American Expeditionary Forces*. London: Abelard-Schuman, 1963.

Leuchtenburg, William E. *Herbert Hoover*. New York: Henry Holt and Company, 2009.

Marshall, S. L. A. *World War I*. Boston, MA: Houghton Mifflin, 2001.

Bibliography

Martin, James Kirby. *America and Its People*. New York: HarperCollins, 1993.

Montefiore, Simon Sebag. *Speeches That Changed the World*. London: Quercus Publishing Place, 2005.

Remini, Robert V. *A Short History of the United States*. New York: Harper Collins Publishers, 2008.

Smith, Carter. *Presidents: Every Question Answered*. New York: Metro Books, 2004.

Smith, Gene. *Until the Last Trumpet Sounds: The Life of General of the Armies John J. Pershing*. New York: John Wiley & Sons, Inc., 1998.

Tindall, George and David Emory Shi. *America, A Narrative History*. New York: W. W. Norton & Company, 1997.

Trask, David. *The AEF and Coalition Warmaking, 1917–1918*. Lawrence: University Press of Kansas, 1993.

Willmott, H. P. *World War I*. New York: DK Publishing, 2003.

Wilson, Woodrow. *Address to the Senate*. July 10, 1919.

Further Resources

Clements, Kendrick A. *Woodrow Wilson: World Statesman.* Chicago, IL: Dee, Ivan R. Publisher, 1999.

Dommermuth-Costa, Carol. *Woodrow Wilson.* Minneapolis, MN: Lerner Publishing Group, 2003.

Elston, Heidi M. D. *Calvin Coolidge: 30th President of the United States.* Edina, MN: ABDO Publishing Company, 2009.

————. *Warren G. Harding: 29th President of the United States.* Edina, MN: ABDO Publishing Company, 2009.

Green, Robert. *World War I.* Farmington Hills, MI: Cengage Gale, 2007.

Heckscher, August. *Woodrow Wilson.* New York: Macmillan Publishing Company, Inc., 1993.

Kyvig, David. *Daily Life in the United States, 1920–1940: How Americans Lived Through the Roaring Twenties and the Great Depression.* Chicago, IL: Dee, Ivan R. Publisher, 2004.

Landau, Elaine. *Warren G. Harding.* Minneapolis, MN: Lerner Publishing Company, 2004.

Matthews, Rubert O. *The Attack on the Lusitania.* New York: Scholastic Library Publishing, 1989.

Pestritto, Ronald J. *Woodrow Wilson and the Roots of Modern Liberalism.* Lanham, MD: Rowman & Littlefield Publishers, Inc., 2005.

Preston, Diana. *Remember the Lusitania!* New York: Walker & Company, 2003.

Ross, Stewart. *World War I.* Mankato, MN: Black Rabbit Books, 2007.

Rumsch, BreAnn. *Woodrow Wilson.* Edina, MN: ABDO Publishing Company, 2009.

Saunders, Nicholas. *World War I: A Primary Source History.* Chicago, IL: Gareth Stevens Publishing, 2005.

Souter, Gerry and Janet. *Warren G. Harding.* Mankato, MN: The Child's World, Inc., 2008.

Web sites

Calvin Coolidge:

http://www.whitehouse.gov/about/presidents/calvincoolidge/

http://www.youtube.com/watch?v=5puwTrLRhmw

History of World War I:

http://www.firstworldwar.com/

http://www.worldwar1.com/

http://www.pbs.org/greatwar/

http://www.bbc.co.uk/history/worldwars/wwone/

Roaring Twenties:

http://www.youtube.com/watch?v=3svvCj4yhYc

Warren Harding:

http://www.whitehouse.gov/about/presidents/WarrenHarding/

http://www.americanpresidents.org/presidents/president.asp?PresidentNumber=28

http://www.youtube.com/watch?v=lL5aZLlfVy4

Woodrow Wilson:

http://www.whitehouse.gov/about/presidents/woodrowwilson/

http://www.pbs.org/wgbh/amex/wilson/

http://www.youtube.com/watch?v=n6nhqFIIGR4

Picture Credits

Index

About the Author

Tim McNeese is associate professor of history at York College in York, Nebraska. Professor McNeese holds degrees from York College, Harding University, and Missouri State University. He has published more than 100 books and educational materials. His writing has earned him a citation in the library reference work, *Contemporary Authors* and multiple citations in *Best Books for Young Teen Readers.* In 2006, Tim appeared on the History Channel program, *Risk Takers, History Makers: John Wesley Powell and the Grand Canyon.* He was been a faculty member at the Tony Hillerman Writers Conference in Albuquerque. His wife, Beverly, is assistant professor of English at York College. They have two married children, Noah and Summer, and three grandchildren—Ethan, Adrianna, and Finn William. Tim and Bev have sponsored college study trips on the Lewis and Clark Trail and to the American Southwest. You may contact Professor McNeese at tdmcneese@york.edu.

About the Consultant

Richard Jensen is Research Professor at Montana State University, Billings. He has published 11 books on a wide range of topics in American political, social, military, and economic history, as well as computer methods. After taking a Ph.D. at Yale in 1966, he taught at numerous universities, including Washington, Michigan, Harvard, Illinois-Chicago, West Point, and Moscow State University in Russia.